JELL-O GIRLS

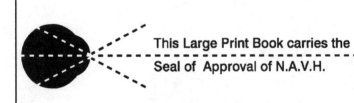

This Large Print Book carries the Seal of Approval of N.A.V.H.

JELL-O GIRLS

A FAMILY HISTORY

ALLIE ROWBOTTOM

THORNDIKE PRESS
A part of Gale, a Cengage Company

Farmington Hills, Mich • San Francisco • New York • Waterville, Maine
Meriden, Conn • Mason, Ohio • Chicago

LIBRARY OF CONGRESS CIP DATA ON FILE.
CATALOGUING IN PUBLICATION FOR THIS BOOK
IS AVAILABLE FROM THE LIBRARY OF CONGRESS

ISBN-13: 978-1-4328-5414-0 (hardcover)

Published in 2018 by arrangement with Little, Brown and Company, a division of Hachette Book Group, Inc.

Printed in the United States of America
1 2 3 4 5 6 7 22 21 20 19 18

AUTHOR'S NOTE

Much of this book is memoir. To write it, I relied on my own present recollections of experiences over time. Elsewhere, I relied on my mother's memory, as recounted to me through the years and as conveyed in her writings. All memories are subjective and affected by time, and I suspect that my mother would be the first to point that out, as well as to offer additions and amendments to the story I've told here. I am confident, though, that I have been true to her own sense of herself and to her story as I came to know them.

Like many memorists, I have chosen to change some names and characteristics, compressed or omitted some events, and re-created dialogue.

For Mary

PROLOGUE

She leaned forward, mouth opened for the wobbling pink Jell-O I steered toward her. *"Here comes the Jell-O train,"* I sing-songed, as if she were a child and I her mother, piloting a spoon into my baby's mouth. She kept her lips closed over a laugh, focused on swallowing, and said nothing.

Across the room the TV flashed images of a Main Street somewhere in America, a dilapidated factory. Faded red brick, a smokestack, and a plaque: *The Jell-O Company, 1900–1964.* My mother gestured, mouth still full, pointing at the screen, suddenly frantic.

"Today we're revisiting LeRoy, New York," the newscaster said. "Birthplace of Jell-O, where, in late 2011 and early 2012, a group of girls suffered mysterious Tourette's-like symptoms with no known cause."

The camera cut to old footage of the girls, seated around a table, twitching, holding their own hands to stop themselves from flailing. Their eyes were rimmed in black liner. Their hair was neatly swept into headbands. Their lips were glossy and pink. Their mothers sat beside them, tensed against the camera's gaze, as if reined in to compensate for their daughters' unbounded bodies.

We had followed the story closely, my mother and I. The mystery of Katie Krautwurst, a senior at LeRoy High School, who, in October 2011, awoke from a nap with her chin frozen. It jutted from her face at an unnatural angle. Her face was in spasm, her whole body twitching. Weeks later, her best friend, Thera, took a nap and woke up similarly altered. She, too, was ticking, throwing her arms, jerking her head, stuttering.

The girls were both popular, both cheerleaders. Both had neatly conformed to the ideal of girlhood in their community, where the football team reigns supreme and Jell-O salads are still served on holidays and at local church potlucks. And the other girls, the girls who followed, also falling asleep, also awakening changed: those girls were cheerleaders, too. But after a while the numbers grew and the symptoms spread. Quiet girls like Lydia Parker were afflicted, too. One girl wasn't a girl at all but a thirty-six-year-old woman, a nurse.

About this "mystery illness" the media said many things. They said *This is how it all started* and then offered theories of train wrecks and toxic spills, black mold in the classrooms, witchcraft in the woods. They said *There is no end in sight* and talked about the diagnosis — conversion disorder, mass psychogenic illness — but always with a disbelieving tone, their faces floating on the television screen, disembodied heads in small side-by-side boxes. On other shows, the girls sat on sofas beside their mothers, answering questions and twitching more violently the more they spoke. "I know my daughter," Thera's mother said. "She's a normal happy girl. There must be something physically wrong with her." The mothers insisted, and the girls all agreed. A refrain emerged: they wanted the world to know they weren't crazy.

"Before this," Thera stuttered, arms flailing as she started to speak, "I was fine." As she convulsed, the other girls began to as well, their movements picking up until the couch was rocked by the violence of their bodies.

■ ■ ■ ■

We weren't afraid of them, though the nation was. In the years approaching my mother's death, she and I were fixated on these girls. We talked about every unfolding aspect of their story. Hours on the phone about their lives, about our lives, about how our histories were entwined, about how we were implicated. How this "mystery illness" was a part of a system of symbolism, one older than us, older than Jell-O, consumerism, and America itself. One older even than witchcraft. One as old as men and women and words. This illness and its attendant metaphors, my mother told me, were what she'd been trying to write about all these years. This, she said, was why she'd started her memoir in the first place.

She pronounced *memoir* with a soft *r* — *memwah* — and talked about hers constantly. In fact, the book, almost as old as I was, sometimes seemed to me like my mother's second child, and I resented her flourished memwah for all the years she spent writing it, all the years she spent away from me. But until I got older, I never thought of her book the way she did: as a spell she wrote to stop her family curse and save herself.

Her writing would reclaim her life story, she believed, and the story of her mother before her. Her writing would become a counter-curse.

We come from Jell-O. It is our birthright, bought by my mother's great-great-uncle by marriage for $450 in 1899 and sold twenty-six years later for $67 million. Jell-O money paid my mother's health insurance. It many times bought my ticket to her bedside in the cancer ward at Mount Sinai, where in the winter of 2015 we watched the girls of LeRoy, searching for glimpses of ourselves.

Even so, my mother rarely ate the stuff. She saw Jell-O as an effigy of a curse she longed to escape. An apron, a kitchen, and long hours spent molding the perfect dessert had always seemed a cage to her, and she dreamed of freedom. Art and travel, music and self-expression, a life sung loudly and lived without fear.

But, sick as she was that winter, Jell-O was all she could keep down. "Who would have thought," she whispered one night as I was feeding her. I pretended not to hear. It hurt too much, to acknowledge every incremental loss she bore on the road to losing her life. I learned to be choosy with my empathy. She smacked her lips in mock satisfaction then, and listed the food she'd eat if she could. Cold slices of pineapple, fried-egg sandwiches, a burger so rare it dripped bloody juices. "You'll get there," I said, coaxing her to take *one more bite.*

Afterward, she slept, her little mouth open, sighs arriving like characters in her dreams, expressions of comfort, maybe, maybe of pain. Her red curls, touched with gray where the dye had worn off, haloed her face. Her hands were open at her sides, waiting for my palm, which molded perfectly to the soft shell of hers. I sat, our fingers interlaced, looking out the window, keeping watch, waiting for her eyes to open. Waiting to hear her voice.

From her room at Mount Sinai, we could see the vented smoke from the Carver Houses' rooftops, colliding with the winter air, making a cloud we hovered above. We could see cabs on Madison Avenue, fluorescent against the gray ground, and dirty bodega awnings, leafless trees like bodies, thin and aching in the cold. I walked the barren city every afternoon, arriving at her bedside with all varieties of liquids and broths, black-cherry Jell-O because she had mumbled through half sleep that it sounded better than the strawberry she received for lunch each day. Peppermint candies for her to suck, never swallow. Wonton soup I carried in a paper sack tucked under my coat and close to my body, to keep the heat in.

That was in January. By March, she'd be back in the hospital, unable to keep her food down, and Jell-O would remain the only thing she could stomach. By June, she would stop treatments and return home to a rented bed in the sunroom, to the hospice care that helped her to a front-row seat at my wedding in the garden, where I married the man I love into the Jell-O legacy. Two months after that, on the first day of September, she would leave me, passing away with the sunrise, unable to the end to talk about death, its cruelty, her fear. Unable to fathom how it was that Jell-O was the last meal she ever ate.

Somehow, though, I was unsurprised by the coincidence of my mother's last meal. I was used to black magic's mean jokes by then. My mother had been sick for decades, always in pain, always bargaining for her health, casting spells to keep herself alive long enough to see me into womanhood, to pass some sort of gauntlet. Once, when

15

cancer had returned and another surgery was imminent, she traveled to Egypt, stood on the bow of a boat, and mimed scooping tumors from her body and throwing them overboard, offerings to the brown Nile water. "It's taken care of," she'd assured me, her voice solemn with the spell she had spoken to the river as she exorcised the cancer from her liver and gut. And she was right. When she returned, CT scans found no sign of the tumors they'd revealed the month before.

At first, the spell stuck. The tumors stayed vanished; she lived. But in time, every spell weakens. This I know. And even though time's dilution of my mother's witchcraft gave way to the cancer that killed her, I am still counting on her magic. Because the spell my mother cast that day slowed the curse she believed had made her sick in the first place, the curse she believed had befallen the girls of LeRoy, the curse she worried was coming for me, too.

The curse. When my mother was a child, it was used to explain all manner of familial misfortune. Death, alcoholism, wealth and the existential boredom it brought with it. It was, she was told, confined to men and therefore nothing for her to worry about.

All she had to do was stay cute, stay pretty, stay silent. Later she understood these admonitions *were* the curse. The curse wasn't confined to men; it came from them, from a social structure predicated on their power. The curse was the silence impressed upon her, her mother before her, and countless women before them. The curse was the sickness that silence becomes when swallowed, lumps of unspoken words ticking like bombs.

Our task was to reclaim and speak, to take up space with our bodies and our voices. *This is how we save ourselves,* my mother constantly reminded me, through words and through witchcraft, that deep, intuitive power alive in every woman, connecting us across space and time. *If you remember nothing else, remember this,* she said. And so, I write. I return to my mother's body, her voice, through the hundreds of pages she left for me, the story I consult now like a spell book, searching its pages for incantations I might hold up against the silence she left behind.

■ ■ ■ ■

BOOK I

■ ■ ■

1

They named my mother Mary. She was born in 1945, the last year of the Second World War. Her father, Bob, was a naval pilot with soft eyes and high cheekbones that cast shadows like smudges across the side of his face. Her mother, Midge, had been a journalist in Honolulu before Bob swept her off her feet. Midge hadn't been sure about children. But they were what one did after marriage, she reasoned. At least she had Bob, and the glamour and travel his profession ensured. She thought about this often, as she dressed in the morning, as she fell asleep at night. What would her life have been like if she'd defied the norm, stayed childless and free? Would she be writing now? She pictured herself at a desk surrounded by books, a cup of coffee steaming, a typewriter recording her words, and her byline, *Mary Jane Fussell,* claiming them. But each morning she woke to the children's cries, drowning out what could have been.

She rose from an empty bed and stayed housebound, adventure just outside her window, too risky for a woman alone. My grandparents lived in Lima, Peru, when my mother was born. There, Bob flew commercial jets for Panagra. He was always working. But he was lucky. While other pilots were drafted to fly dangerous jungle routes, waiting for shots to ring out, Bob kept the perks of his prewar profession: the shiny green-and-gold winged globe pin, the white hat, the black leather shoes he shined himself before each flight. He told jokes over the intercom, he smiled wide and white as passengers disembarked, he shook their hands, held their babies. Flight was still remarkable then, and a handsome pilot was a celebrity to most people.

Mary was born on the first day of spring. The March heat settled like a wet blanket over Midge while she held her dark-haired daughter in a bare-walled hospital room, listening to the whir of the fan, watching the light change outside, pulling night down over the city. Bob had left yellow roses on the bedside table, a glass of water, a book.

They pulsed there, reminders of her incapacity.

For Midge, pregnancy had been uncomfortable. She'd known, from the birth of her first child three years before, what to expect, but her mother had written that it would be easier the second time. It wasn't. She hated her fat ankles, her unwieldy body, which she wanted to exit as she would a poorly lit room.

With both children, the labor pains had arrived like relief, like the promise of a life she might reclaim, and Midge had eagerly fetched her prepacked bag of toiletries and clothes and climbed into the car Bob wheeled slowly to the hospital. When they arrived, she walked through the doors Bob held open for her, climbed onto a gurney, and politely deferred to the team of white-suited doctors who stood at her bedside, telling her what was happening. "You're going to have a baby, Mrs. Fussell," they said in thick accents, as if she didn't know. "Are you ready for your medicine?" She nodded. Then the nurse arrived, administered, and twilight fell over Midge, who in the space between day and night saw her daughter enter the world as a shadow.

Midge had hoped her second child would

balance out the needs of Thomas, her first. They'd have each other, she reasoned, and could lean more on each other and less on her. The thought of this, the promise of this freedom, carried her through the physical discomfort of pregnancy. After Mary's birth, Midge watched for the relief she'd been promised by baby books, her mother. She sat by her window, waiting for lightness to fall back into her life. She waited for the light, she waited for her husband, anticipating his return each evening like the ringing of a bell, the filling of a glass. They ate out, sometimes, at the country club, with friends from Panagra. This was the best part of Midge's life in Lima, the night.

A year passed. Mornings stayed endless, colorless, full of boring minutiae — groceries to be ordered, a baby to burp and feed, a mess to clean up, a toddler to comfort when he cried. Each day the city moved on outside Midge's windows, and she listened for it hungrily: honking horns, whistles and shouts; the sound of vendors ringing bells, of cart wheels over dirt or cobblestone. Each day they called out *Mango!,* held up wet, yellow blossoms Midge longed to taste. But she never felt free enough to do so. Even when the children napped, their *ni-*

ñera keeping watch by the window in their bedroom, fanning herself with a stiff pleat of paper glued to a stick, Midge never pursued the things she needed, the things that made her whole. Never did she feed paper into the typewriter she'd once used to write stories for the local paper, for anything other than letters home. Never did she push out her chair and take her housecoat off, hang it on a hook, pick up her purse, and walk out the door. Never did she try that cadmium fruit, bite to its seedy heart.

Midge had been married once before, to a man — a boy, really — who drank too much and made crass, critical remarks. It was a quick, impulsive union, a desperate attempt to depart from LeRoy, where she could barely stand to be, the scandal of her father's affairs — the latest with the choir leader of the Methodist Congregation, a mousy woman he ran off with to Florida — rippling out from his absence. But her first husband turned out to be from the same mold as her father. Only a week after the wedding, he stayed out late after work and returned smelling of another woman, indignant when Midge asked him where he'd been.

Was she truly so undesirable? Wanted only for her money? Were all men pre-programmed to cheat, lie, leave? Either way, Midge told herself, she wouldn't enable men's childishness. The second time her husband failed to return home, she picked up the phone, called her mother, and told her with a measured, businesslike tone what she needed to do. It would be a scandal, but both women had grown used to hushed gossip, whisperings of their failures and faults, whatever they had done or not done to drive the patriarch of their family into the choir leader's arms.

So within a week they'd packed their suitcases and boarded a plane for Reno. It was January, cool enough for furs. Mother and daughter donned their best coats and strolled arm in arm through the casinos, chatting, making bets, ordering drinks. When they returned home to LeRoy, it was as the recipients of two quickie divorces.

Despite the talk around town, after her divorce Midge had felt free. And with Bob, whom she met a few years later, when she moved to Honolulu, she felt treasured in a way that assured her he'd never leave. Bob was different from the men from home, men like her father who rarely spoke and hid behind their papers, their glasses of bourbon. He was lighter, lighthearted. He stood in tiki bars with his hands in the pockets of his khaki trousers, leaning back on his heels and laughing, looking at her. He twirled her on the dance floor, his hand in the dip of her upper back, pressing into the space between her shoulder blades, her wings.

This was everything she wanted, Midge had thought in the early months of her marriage to Bob: to be desired. But now, saddled with two babies, she felt stripped of the self she'd once been, peeled and reduced to a core, a body changed by pregnancy into an object of shame. Once, on a rare afternoon with Bob, when Mary was four months old and Tom was almost three, Midge sat in the front seat of a little rented car Bob wheeled around sharp turns, steep inclines, climbing into the Andes in low gear, the children wedged into the back on either side of a picnic basket. When the family stopped for lunch, Midge spread out blankets and unpacked the egg salad sandwiches she'd prepared that morning. She sat, exhausted, with Mary in her lap, watching Bob hold Tom up to point out the rusting carcass of a passenger train, cars scattered like limbs in the valley below.

When the children began to cry, Midge and Bob packed them back into the car.

Midge braced as the winding path back down the mountain rocked her family back and forth, as baby Mary straddled her, vomiting repeatedly onto her shoulder, down her back, across the front of her blouse. Each time, with each hiccup, each sob, Midge stripped away another piece of soggy clothing until she wore only her bra and panties. Bob laughed, his eyes on the narrow road, and removed one hand to playfully pinch the side of her stomach, once drawn into a firm cord of muscle and now doughy. He meant it as a joke, but Midge felt mortified. She feared she'd lost what had made her lovable; her body, the object of her husband's desire, had changed — it belonged now to her children. Even her thoughts were suffocated by their screams. She looked down, down at her wailing baby, down at herself, her painful breasts, made conical by her brassiere, into which Mary's body melded. There was no privacy in this life. No space just for her, her thoughts, her words.

Once home Bob went inside ahead of the others and returned with a housecoat for his wife to wear in from the car. Midge wrapped the quilted fabric around herself, handed Mary to her husband, and climbed from the car, the baby screaming, arms outstretched, wanting to return to her mother's body. *I need a moment,* Midge said to Bob, *give me just a moment,* as she walked inside and into the bathroom, shutting the door, silence embracing her.

2

Once upon a delightfully light and wholesome dream, Jell-O and America fell in love
and lived happily ever after in marketing
heaven. But, as in all great love stories, first
there was transformation, and a journey.

Long before Jell-O crossed oceans and
landed in LeRoy, it was known just as
gelatin, a product confined to the kitchens
of European royalty, less a convenience
product than a luxury. Throughout the
fifteenth century, gelatin molds ornamented
the feasts of kings and aristocrats. Napoleon
Bonaparte, Marie de Médicis, and Richard
the Second were all reported to have enjoyed the gelatin desserts prepared for them.
In the Victorian era, the trend persisted; the
ability to mold gelatin into decorative
shapes appealed to the ornate aesthetic
sensibilities of the time. By the nineteenth
century, gelatin had finally found America
and its people, and even Thomas Jefferson

enjoyed a fancy gelatin mold at his Monticello feasts. But the work of scalding hooves, extracting and skimming fat, and adding flavor always fell to servants and took long hours of hard labor. There was always meticulous effort and human pain involved in its production.

At least, that is, until 1845, when Peter Cooper — creator of Cooper Union, the Tom Thumb locomotive, and a gas-powered "flying machine" that partly blinded him — patented unflavored gelatin, which he sold primarily to commercial kitchens. Cooper, who also produced glue to fund his more adventurous ventures, put little energy into marketing or sales. While he worked to lay wire beneath the Atlantic, a LeRoy businessman named Pearle Wait worked to make gelatin attractive to independent consumers.

Mr. Wait and his wife, May, made cough syrup and laxatives. But they barely got by, so Pearle spent hours in the basement, tinkering with formulas, trying to perfect a mix of gelatin and flavor. The result was Jell-O's first prototype, which was made almost entirely of sugar. But nobody seemed to mind. Its taste was the slipperiest sweet, and it was nutritious, too! Good for the gut, hair, skin, and nails!

May tackled the look of it: she began to experiment with the different shapes it might take, setting it in squares, then circles, just for fun. The Waits added an *O* to the name of their creation so that it matched Grain-O, a "pure food drink" billed as a coffee alternative for both children and adults, and then sold Jell-O to the drink's manufacturer, Midge's great-uncle-in-law, Orator Francis Woodward. The price tag for his purchase was $450: the modern-day equivalent of $4,000.

I have read that Pearle Wait went bankrupt soon after he sold Jell-O, after the Woodward fortune, already sizable, doubled, then tripled, after America's Most Famous Dessert sold box after box and piled into the cabinets of every kitchen in America, stacking up like so many clean white bricks. But it wasn't luck that put it there, in the pantry, in the icebox, on the plate. It was Orator. A self-made man who had earned his fortune on patent medicines and fake nest eggs treated to de-lice henhouses, Orator was versed in the work needed to grow a product. When he bought the Jell-O patent, signing his name above Mr. Wait's on a contract that hangs now in the Jell-O Museum in LeRoy, he thought he might as well give this little product everything he had, give it every chance to succeed.

So Orator traded his Grain-O for Jell-O, replacing silos and sifters with barrels of sugar and sacks of powdered gelatin, shipped in from factory farms. Trucks arrived each week heaped with the dusty remnants of tissue and bone, ready to be mixed with sweetness and dye to make the first Jell-O flavors — strawberry, raspberry, orange, or lemon.

Animal parts were plentiful, as was sugar, but initially, Jell-O sales were slow. LeRoy myth says that Orator, exasperated by poor profits, once tried to sell Jell-O's patent to his plant superintendent for thirty-five dollars. But nobody was buying. So Orator implemented every plan he could to move his product: on quiet weekday midmornings, he sent his handsomest marketing men to suburban front doors to flash white teeth and hold out white boxes to the women who answered. Immigrants en route to America were served Jell-O for dessert; when they landed at Ellis Island and walked shakily to solid ground, it was to be rewarded with promise and newness and a metal mold, round and ridged and just like all the others, *Jell-O* etched upon it in cheerful text.

By 1902, Jell-O was manufactured just

down the street from Orator's house, the river outside the factory running colorful and sweet, changing color weekly depending on the flavor. Everyone in LeRoy worked for Jell-O. Parents packed powder into wax-paper pouches, which were then sealed and slipped into red-and-white boxes. Some put on suits and went to work in the offices at the front of the factory, or in Rochester, or Manhattan, where Jell-O's advertising agency was headquartered. Franklin King was one such man.

An ad-man artist, King worked for Dauchy Company, the agency in charge of marketing the dessert. By 1904, he was frustrated by slow sales and looking for a new marketing campaign. So, in the confection's first brilliant marketing twist, King staged a series of pictures featuring his own towheaded daughter Elizabeth preparing and enjoying Jell-O. The photographs ushered in a boost in sales, and the Dauchy agency eagerly sent Elizabeth King one hundred empty Jell-O boxes to replace her wooden blocks. After that, Elizabeth's parents produced weekly photo shoots, during which Elizabeth would appear in a new outfit, enacting a new scenario with her Jell-O box toys.

Little Elizabeth's performance of young

girlhood was vital to the product's success. The brand's aesthetic, still establishing itself, rested precariously on the impossibility of her aging. So, when Elizabeth turned eight and threatened to outgrow her alter ego, her father brought her into the office and had her stand, pretending to hold a teakettle, while Rose O'Neill, designer of the Kewpie dolls, sketched the lines of her body and drew a box of Jell-O into the frame of her fingertips.

In that moment, the Jell-O girl was immortalized. She became forever a child, stitched to the polka dot dress, buckled into her black shoes, holding out a silver platter of Jell-O — offering, inviting. In the early ad campaigns that ran in *Ladies' Home Journal,* she is alternatingly demure and feisty. Sometimes she politely offers Jell-O to her mother's guests. Sometimes she sneaks into the pantry and pulls down a box, pours colored crystals into a bowl, adds water, and stirs. *So easy even a child can do it!* the advertisement proclaims. At Christmastime, the Jell-O girl adds candied cherries to the mix while Mother fetches Daddy a drink, and then it's *Surprise!* and everyone is so happy to have saved room on their plate.

In old images, her eyes are small, set deep into the bones of her face. She looks cheery, but not overly so. In some reprints, some copies of old newspaper ads, black ink intended as shadow has subsumed her eyes entirely, so that two dark sockets puncture her face like holes. I grew up knowing that her smallness and her silence were what made her sweet. I grew up knowing that this was true for me, too. I considered her a part of me, but now I consider her an emblem of something much larger: a silence that sickens.

3

Lima, 1948. Cocktails at the club to discuss leaving Peru, returning to LeRoy. There, Midge argued, Bob might work for her aunt Edith, ensure an excessive inheritance; there Midge might feel at home.

The ceiling fans turned slowly, like airplane propellers winding down after a flight. Midge held the thin stem of her martini glass, looked down at the olive in its belly. She was exhausted. The children still felt like weight, heavier now than in pregnancy, where at least they'd been silent. The chatter of their bickering thickened in her brain, congealing. Oh, how she had wanted to write. To travel the world unencumbered. She hadn't expected it would be so hard to do so — she'd pictured children as easy accessories to her adventures. But now she was confined to routines, to the house — she could be anywhere, and all she would see was the inside of her own home. She looked over the table at Bob, going on about the logistics of a move, the pros and cons of it, the dangers of losing their independence. Once she had wanted him in every city in the world. Now the memory of desire was like an erased word: faint gray marks where before there had been black.

Midge was in mourning for the life she'd dreamed of. There was a life out there she'd almost had. She'd thought she wanted to be wanted, but now she wanted to be heard. But her grief was unutterable, even to her husband. Motherhood was supposed to be joyous. Everything she'd ever read or watched about being a woman had promised her this, and she'd believed it. And yet here she was, trapped, silenced, her identity subsumed. No longer was she witty Midge, the beautiful writer and dancer and lover of art. She was just *Mother, Momma, Mommy.* Every day she spent housebound, placating, pleasing, perfecting recipes out of boredom, every day compounded the urge to flee, to find the self she'd been before. She felt it bodily, a fluttering behind her sternum, a trapped sparrow, flapping its wings in vain. She knew it was hopeless. She knew there was no solution. What difference did it make if she lived in Lima or LeRoy? At least at home she'd have her mother. Her cousins.

Aunt Edith. The nearness of inheritance and the ease of wealth.

She shifted in her seat, slid her empty glass toward the edge of the table, scanning for the waiter. The band began a ballroom rumba. She could fall asleep right here. Bob reached across the white tablecloth and flipped his palm open for hers. She wouldn't say no. Tension between them was another exhaustion to avoid. She wiggled her body off the banquette and followed her husband to the floor.

And so by springtime it was decided. They would go. They packed their things and left Peru. This was the right decision, Midge was sure of it. Her children would live in the house on East Main Street where she'd grown up. They'd play hide-and-seek in the dumbwaiters, as she and her brother had; they'd fall asleep in their own bedrooms, Mary's with the angel-shaped crack on the ceiling. They'd wake each morning to lemon light warming their cheeks, streaming through their bedroom windows, both with perfect views of the perfect golf course, its trimmed, smooth green unfurling like soft cotton, the finest fabric. They would have a perfect childhood, self-sufficient and safe, and she would finally have time to herself.

■ ■ ■ ■

In LeRoy, Bob spent his days outside, overseeing Edith's farms. Midge remained situated in the house. Her life revolved now around board membership on community organizations, the weekly menu — which she planned out every Monday with Elfrida, the maid — and cocktail hour at five sharp, every night. Drinking quickly became the best part of Midge's life. It freed her from boredom, carving out the space she'd craved for herself in Peru. And it was social. Her cousins, Ann and Betty, lived around the corner. Her mother and aunt, just up the hill. Edith's grandchildren, Joan and John, often drove in from Rochester. The house was always full.

This was what Midge had hoped for in moving back: a partial return to the self she'd been before the tight constraints of motherhood had reduced her. It was the best she could hope for. Work and writing would always be an impropriety, now that she was a married mother of two. But at least in LeRoy she could be herself socially; at least now her voice could be used for laughter and not just hushed admonishments. Maybe she overdid it a little. Most nights she started with gin and tonics and switched to bourbons, winding up on Bob's lap, his hands casually on her waist, before dinner and bed. Most mornings she reached for the bottle of aspirin on her bedside table. But the children were fine, she reasoned, self-sufficient here in LeRoy, where childhood worked best as a prepackaged product, a convenience. While the adults drank, the kids played, safe on their own in the streets, Tom riding his bike, Mary shouting *Wait up!* in his wake. It was only Elfrida, the maid-turned-nanny, who could call them home. Each night her bellow sounded out the back door, a commanding dinner bell.

Elfrida lifted Midge's responsibilities from her like they were feather light, the children nothing more than overnight bags, easily unpacked. Every day she occupied Mary with work, pinching the perimeters of the pie crusts, creasing ridges into round edges, pouring goopy fruit or creamy Jell-O pudding into the belly of the pan.

"I've got a girl at home just like her," Elfrida told Midge one afternoon, gesturing to Mary, engrossed in pressing a cookie cutter into a sheet of dough, producing an assembly of triangle-skirted women, each one identical.

Midge nodded, said something to acknowledge Elfrida's life outside the kitchen. But she worried this might make her uncomfortable. Elfrida rarely spoke about herself — it wouldn't have been proper. But perhaps, Midge thought, she stayed so private because she wanted a separation, a distance between East Main Street and her home, on the other side of the train tracks, a small white house packed full of girls. Midge knew Elfrida saw her children rarely, that she missed them while she worked, long hours cleaning and baking and entertaining Mary and Tom, rich little dumplings who waged petty wars against each other. She knew but did nothing about it, aside from Christmas bonuses and Sundays off. This was just how things were, her wealthy woman's mind reasoned. Everyone had their curses to bear, and Elfrida's blackness was hers.

Mary was raised to understand the injustice Elfrida faced, but she still sentimentalized her, imagining her love as real. It was an unembarrassed whiteness she would carry into her adult life, immortalizing both Midge and Elfrida in her memoir less as real people than as superficial emblems of race and class. *My archetypal black earth mother,* she wrote, *my elegant white goddess.*

The Woodwards were revered in LeRoy, and so they were constantly surveilled, their comings and goings often gracing the pages of the *LeRoy Gazette*'s society column. Around town, their name and money were everywhere: the airport, the factory, the municipal building, the Woodward mausoleum, which stood on its own in a shady part of the cemetery, a whole building made of granite with a Tiffany window nestled into the peak of the roof. And of course the Woodward Memorial Library, a large colonial building that looked like a temple.

None of these buildings had much to do with her, Mary thought. They were testaments to her family's Jell-O fortune, but even that felt distant, belonging more to Aunt Edith than to her. But the buildings, the money, the pomp and circumstance around the Woodwards, mortified Tom. In a town otherwise enamored with normality, nine-to-five factory jobs, and three square meals a day, he hated the difference of his family's wealth. Each time he and Mary so much as caught a cold, news of their condition was published in the *Gazette: Master Thomas and Mistress Mary Fussell fell ill this week and were absent from school but are*

recovering nicely and should return Monday.
Afternoons when Aunt Edith, concerned it
was too cold for walking, sent Marshall the
driver to ferry the children home from
school in the shiny black limousine, Mary
pranced toward it like a movie star while
Tom hid beneath his scarf and slid surrepti-
tiously into the humming car, knowing
everyone was watching.

To Mary the perks of wealth were easy and
fun, as light and delightful as the Jell-O
LeRoy loved. So she couldn't understand
why her family seemed stuck. They had
everything, after all. Mansions and farmland
and fur coats. But in LeRoy, it was as if the
Woodwards were trapped inside a gelatinous
mound of money that jiggled when you
poked it but never broke. Mary pictured
her entire family stuck inside this mold, like
peas and carrots, or candied cherries, or
pieces of pineapple and peach.
    Later she'd say the Woodwards had made
a bargain for their money, and in so doing
they had seduced their own despair, buying
into the myth of patriarchy by building a
fortune predicated on the myth of domesticity and the reduction of a woman's worth
to her culinary concoctions. Because of this,
she wrote, the family would always be

miserable inside their wealth, stuck in their antiquated ideals, their alcoholism, and the small town of LeRoy, itself suffocated by the thick immobility of the product it had birthed. But at the time, little Mary didn't see all this. And though she enjoyed the trappings of her privilege, she hated the dullness of LeRoy, everything the same, sleepy and safe. Even as she aged out of first grade, then second, then third, even as she made friends and learned to ride her bike, she didn't forget the Lima of her birth. She was only three when they'd left, but she remembered the colors there: mango yellow, cayenne-pepper red. In LeRoy everything was beige stone, white paint. The town hall and the Unitarian Church, the storefronts on Main Street. The snow that came each December, falling in unending layers. Colorless, noiseless, it was pushed and shoveled and packed into walls so high that when Mary looked out the window, there was nothing. Everything had been erased.

Out of boredom, then, or perhaps desperation, Mary began to follow after Tom and his troupe of friends on weekdays after school. She was elated when they agreed, finally, to play hide-and-seek with her, only to cruelly leave her crouched behind some shrub while they went home to belly flop on the living room rug and watch Roy Rogers until suppertime. They called her *fatty fatty two-by-four* but later began to hold roller-skating parties for her and her girlfriends in the basement. One day, the boys ran the gramophone cord to the foot of the basement steps so that as everyone skated round and round, wheeling over the polished concrete, Billy Ward and His Dominoes sang "I'd Be Satisfied." At first it was all great fun. But a few of Tom's friends had a trick to play: abruptly, the music cut and the lights went out. Tiny toes pressed down to stop. Mary looked around in the dark, and suddenly a voice said: "I'm right beside you, hold my hand." And then the darkness filled with the shrieks of little girls, fingers wrapped around flaccid little-boy dicks.

4

It was through luck and marriage that my family came into Jell-O money. Midge's aunt Edith married Orator Woodward's son Ernest in 1903, the year before Jell-O sales spiked and sent the Jell-O girl's image and the product she hawked into every home in America. To keep up with sales, the Woodwards expanded the factory on North Street, and Jell-O advertisements were supplemented with a series of recipe booklets featuring classic nursery rhymes and fairy tales rewritten to incorporate the dainty dessert. Branding became an exercise in fable fabrication and real world building. In these new narratives, Mary Mary Quite Contrary grows *silver bells and cockle shells and rows of sweet Jell-O,* and Rip Van Winkle doesn't sleep for ages in the Catskill Mountains but rather eats bowls and bowls of Jell-O administered by a group of gnomes. These books evolved into a series of travelogues featuring the Jell-O girl touring the world with her parrot, Polly, who perches on her outstretched hand or rounded shoulder. The Jell-O girl sees Niagara Falls, the Grand Canyon, and California. She rides a mule to the belly of Yosemite, Polly on the horn of her saddle. She poses in a snowsuit on the Alaskan tundra and dons native garb in Holland, Hawaii, and Russia, always having the *Most Famous* adventures.

A similar booklet, *Desserts of the World,* pushes American fabulism further, bemoaning the fate of foreign housewives, *called upon to serve a dessert at a moment's notice,* who, *know[ing] nothing about Jell-O,* fail miserably. They didn't know! How could they? Jell-O was an all-American dessert, from an all-American town. It was a product of *American* work ethic, *American* science. Advertisements reflected not only nationalistic pride but also an awareness of the country's shifting socioeconomic landscape. And the country *was* shifting, quickly now. As maids and nannies and cooks abandoned their positions in the kitchens of the middle class to work the assembly lines of factories like Jell-O, the responsibilities of American housewives grew.

Ernest Woodward had been well aware of this shift. He'd engineered it, setting up an assembly line at the Jell-O factory in LeRoy, paying workers the best wage in town, plucking them like strawberries, raspberries, oranges, and lemons from their previous jobs in the kitchens of the American middle class and setting them down in rows of sweet Jell-O. These colorful rows were a grand place for the people of LeRoy, the best option available for hardworking individuals looking to support their families. One could almost *hear* the money whirring into existence, as if each box that passed inspection, each packet of powder sealed safely shut, was a stand-in for a thick roll of fragrant green paper. *This* was the American dream! Conveyor belts of cash! A steady stream of employment bringing prosperity to all, regardless of their background.

This steadiness in particular was important to LeRoy residents. By the time Orator bought Jell-O, in 1899, the town had already undergone the gain and traumatic loss of its first and only university, which just happened to be the country's first university for women. Founded by a pair of sisters in

1837, and situated on East Main Street, Ingham University enrolled 117 women in its first summer and graduated thousands before its closure, in 1892. Just fifty-five years after Ingham was founded, financial hardship forced the university to shutter its doors. The furniture and classroom supplies were sold at auction. The buildings were reduced to rubble. From the bricks of the razed dormitories came a new bridge on Main Street. From the stone of the prodigious art conservatory, the Woodward Library was built, with Jell-O money.

The disappearance of "the help" from the homes of the American middle class saw many women entering the kitchen alone for the first time. What to do? The recipes their mothers had handed down were antiquated now, incompatible with modern food technology, which privileged artificiality and imitation. A whole chicken, plucked and washed, was unclean. Potatoes boiled with the skin still on? Dirty.

Tentatively they phoned their local grocer, unsure of what to order. How much sugar did they need each month? How much butter and flour? Timidly they crept to the cupboard to see what they could make. It all seemed so complicated, so many ingredients needed for even the simplest recipe. But wait! What's this? A perfect cardboard box, red lettered and unimposing. *So easy even a child can do it.*

So easy even a *barefooted black boy* can do it. In a 1922 advertisement he stands, potbelly protruding, white teeth gleaming, on the threshold of a freshly painted porch, fluorescent white beneath his feet, offering a simple orange mold to a doughy and delighted Southern mistress. *Oh my!* she pantomimes, hands up in excitement. *Mammy sent dis ovah,* says the boy, the caption beneath him proclaiming that Jell-O was not only delicious enough to meet the standards of *The Big House* but also *appealing enough to turn the sinful of any color away from his neighbor's melon patch.*

Jell-O, the great equalizer. It molded itself easily to any social class. Except, perhaps, a class that might reject campaigns built on racism, nationalism, and sexism. But in early-twentieth-century America, few consumers took up these kinds of issues. Besides, advertisements assured, Jell-O was equally at home in mansions and tract houses. *The butler serves and the housewife too!* All the recipes you'd ever need to class up your mold, available in these darling *Jell-O and the Kewpies* booklets, now in

51

French, German, Swedish, and Yiddish. Bottom line, the Jell-O Company was eager to recruit new consumers.

This was why, in the early 1900s, Jell-O commissioned America's favorite artist, Norman Rockwell, to illustrate a series of cookbooks and advertisements. One of his first illustrations graces the cover of a Yiddish recipe book, the image of a prim, white-haired grandmother pouring boiling water into a bowl of Jell-O powder, bordered by Hebrew script. The Jell-O girl herself was next on Rockwell's list. But the artist, accustomed to painting boys, was technically challenged by her little-girl body (no bosom to speak of). He wound up painting her wearing a floor-length apron. *He erased the lines of her,* my mother, an artist obsessed with painting Rubenesque women, would have said.

This was early in Rockwell's career. He had just started painting covers for the *Saturday Evening Post,* most of which concerned themselves with kitschy renderings of the softer side of World War I, for which he'd been an official military artist. Men's bodies abounded; they were Rockwell's bread and butter. He was the patron saint of soldiers returning home to women and warm houses, the hearth, America and its

Most Famous Dessert! Maybe this is what made Rockwell such a flop with serious critics, such a success with everyday Americans. Even today, Rockwell's work is considered *light!* and *wholesome!,* a throwback, like Jell-O itself, to a simpler time, one we search for wistfully on the internet, scrolling through shrines to nostalgia and decades long past.

The sentimentality of Rockwell's work limited the range of activities available to his female subjects. These women were not Ingham University graduates, nor were they artists themselves; these were women who dreamed only of prom dates and Jell-O molds, white weddings and motherhood. These were the women the Jell-O Company wanted to sell to. So, as the company had with the Jell-O girl, as it would for years to come, it commissioned Rockwell to mold the ideal Jell-O consumer from a list of prescribed attributes American women had learned to revere.

Teaching women, it turns out, was a tenet of Jell-O's marketing. Door-to-door salesmen *taught* housewives what to do with America's Most Famous Dessert. Advertisements carefully explained the preparation process: *Dissolve one packet into one pint of*

53

boiling water. Pour into mold and set in a cool place to harden. Later advertisements featured specific recipes or suggested consumers send away for the rhyming booklets full of them. How sweet and cunning these booklets were, teaching women all over America how to make the perfect Christmas fruit mold, Cherry Cheese Charmer, cranberry squares; teaching women how to mold their Jell-O, so pliable, so good; teaching them how to mold themselves to match it, pliable and good.

Almost as soon as Jell-O arrived on the market, consumers came up with new ways to use it. Jell-O as a salad ingredient, although never before considered, would forever change the face of American veggie consumption. One of the first published gelatin salad recipes, Perfection Salad — a simple mix of coleslaw suspended in an orb of lemon gelatin — debuted in 1905 when its creator, Mrs. John E. Cooke, entered it in a recipe contest sponsored by Knox gelatin. It was a sight to behold, this Perfection Salad. It was self-contained and clean. It sparkled lemon gold when the light hit it just right.

It wasn't long before Cooke's recipe inspired a bevy of Jell-O salads. They filled cookbooks, replacing plain old lettuce almost entirely. They catapulted lemon Jell-O from the fourth to the second bestselling flavor.

Jell-O salads, it turned out, were the perfect place to hide leftovers and stretch the contents of a meager cupboard. And they were cheap. All of which drew the attention of Postum. With Orator and his wife dead and gone, Ernest and Edith decided to sell. The resulting deal, an exchange of Jell-O stock worth $67 million, launched the Woodwards into superwealth.

Postum changed little about Jell-O's production, and perhaps because of this, the Woodwards, and the town of LeRoy, remained synonymous with the brand. The factory still churned out boxes and boxes — even more after the sale. As Postum went about acquiring a roster of other convenience-food products — which eventually prompted the company to change its name to General Foods — Jell-O's popularity grew, as did its affordability. In 1926, Jell-O went from ten cents per box to a special three-for-twenty-five-cent deal.

Initially the move was profitable, but it also ushered in a flock of store-brand competitors. This was the Depression era. Every cent counted, and Jell-O sales declined radically in the early 1930s. The solution was a radio program, *The Cooking School of the Air,* which aired midday on NBC's Red Network. Each fifteen-minute lesson was presided over by Mrs. Frances Lee Barton, a professional home economist employed by General Foods to walk listeners through the construction of Jell-O molds. The trusty old Perfection Salad was featured, as were other, newer concoctions, such as the Jell-O cheese loaf (lemon Jell-O mixed with a spreadable cheese of your choosing and molded into an oblong shape) and the Under the Sea Salad, a mix of canned pears and cream cheese, molded to form a thick base and then topped in lime, the result a green-and-white tower flecked with hints of the fruit stuck inside.

As grotesque as Barton's recipes seem today, at the time nary an eyebrow was lifted. Her Depression-era audience was hungry for something different, something *new,* something *imitation* and now in six delicious flavors. Clearly, the old ways weren't working. Clearly something had failed. The solution was a *new* way of eating. New methods of producing and consuming food: scientifically, conveniently, and according to instruction.

■ ■ ■ ■

Even with so much innovation and cultural interest, the onslaught of cheaper brands, combined with economic depression, kept Jell-O sales sluggish. Electric refrigeration also had something to do with Jell-O's popularity or lack thereof, briefly confining the dessert to a signifier of those who owned refrigerators and those who did not. Although Jell-O could be made in the sink, root cellar, or icebox, those with the most consistent molds obviously didn't have to rely on such antiquated cooling techniques.

It wasn't until the late 1940s that refrigerators with separate deep-freeze units — which cut Jell-O prep time in half — went into mass production, and I imagine Midge waiting for weeks after returning to LeRoy for hers to arrive. In the meantime there was the old icebox, the same unit she remembered from her girlhood, kept out in the garage. Each day she waited for her new unit was another day Elfrida greeted the iceman, fitting the plate of frozen water into the cool locker full of food. Even after the fancy white refrigerator arrived, transforming Midge's kitchen into a modern wonder fit to congeal all the Jell-O she could eat, the icebox stayed in the garage, stocked with beer for Bob. He'd fork a cool bottle between his fingers on his way inside and carry it up to the shower, emerging twenty minutes later pine scented and ready for cocktail hour, a Johnny Mathis record on the player, macadamia nuts in little crystal dishes, fresh ice at the bar, and bourbon to be poured.

5

An autumn afternoon in Edith's mansion, early dusk, the sun recumbent in the sky outside. Warm lamplight filtered into the parlor, and the rhythm of the grandmother clock paced out the distance between twilight and night. Mary and Tom sat side by side on the blue couch, twelve-year-old Tom's feet just touching the floor, nine-year-old Mary's hovering above it, the bow in her frizzy hair lopsided and skewed. Across from them, Midge's cousin John, Edith's grandson, stared blankly into his glass of bourbon, his jaw set as if he were considering something serious.

John was tall, like Bob, but younger, his face soft, his skin smooth. Everything about him seemed boyish, early in his manhood, still twenty-something, still establishing how he fit in his own body. But he was handsome, newly married to a beautiful woman named Jessie, who wore her brunette hair scooped back in pearl barrettes. The two made a striking couple. When they entered a room together, everyone looked up and smiled. Only sometimes did John seem so distant, staring into empty space as if he were looking into a room nobody else could see.

"Our family is cursed, you know," he said abruptly, returning to the parlor. He took a sip of his whiskey, reached forward to flick ash from the cigarette scissored between the fingers of his right hand. "What do you mean?" said Tom, trying to look calm.

John smiled. "It's called the Jell-O curse," he said, staring at Mary, who for an instant thought he looked less handsome than wolfish, like the big bad beast in her Tiny Golden Book rendition of *The Three Little Pigs,* the one Midge had bought her at the supermarket on a rare shopping trip together. "All of the men," John continued, "all of them have been tragic. Train wrecks, actually. They rarely live past forty."

"What happens to them?" Tom asked.

John shrugged. "The curse happens, that's what," he said. He leaned in. "Want to know what the curse is?"

The children nodded.

"Money." He slouched back in his chair and pulled at his cigarette. "Money and its attendant problems," he said, waving at the smoke he exhaled. "The women who chase it, for one." He gestured with his glass in the direction of the parlor, where Jessie was looking at fabric swatches with Edith and Midge.

The children stared at him, confused. His description of the curse was abstract and unclear. But in years to come, it would haunt my mother, who came to fear the curse *because* she was a woman, not despite it. The curse, she told me, was the very attitude Cousin John — like most men — took toward women, an attitude reflected by the messages about women and their worth that her family sold with each box of Jell-O. The curse was the myth that the love and approval of a man like John was something to be earned, something that would bring us women all the happiness we could ever dream of. This myth was, my mother believed, particularly strong in LeRoy, the culture of which was so small-minded and nostalgic and terrified of change that it pressured women into prescribed roles, stifling their voices and making them sick.

As a child, though, Mary was told she was exempt. She was safe, *protected* by the men in her world. "Don't worry, Mona," Cousin John said, "I'll keep you safe." But what

61

happened when he was gone? She thought of her uncle Frank, who, two years earlier, facing financial hardship brought on by two divorces and ill-advised spending, had plummeted off the roof of the Sheraton. His death had been a confirmation of exactly what John was speaking of, the long-held idea among the Woodwards that the curse killed all the *men* in their family. It wasn't just the idea of losing John that lodged itself icily into my mother's young heart; it was her terror that, though she was a girl, the curse would get her, too. That she'd be the first to break the mold.

Cousin John scared Mary, but she loved him, loved the thin wave of excitement that shot up her spine each time he called her Mona. "And what about you, Mona," he'd say whenever she showed up at his side, the top of her head level with his waist. He'd reach down and run his hands through her curls as if he were petting some favored object. "You're marriage material, Mona," he'd say. "If I weren't already taken, I'd scoop you up this instant." He'd wink at her, and she'd smile shyly, gazing up his long torso to his face — handsome, she thought, like a movie star's — and the perfect sweep of his dark-blond hair, which caught the light and shone.

Around Cousin John, Mary imagined herself desired, a femme fatale like the women she saw in the movies. She imagined herself in furs and dresses that hugged her body scandalously tight. And she would have a ring, Mary decided. Not a ruby, like her mother, but a yellow diamond, a canary rimmed in white. She would wear it proudly, showing it off all over the world, which she would travel like an actress, an artist, someone free from the confines of a small town like LeRoy.

In 1955, Aunt Edith died and Mary turned ten. She began to fake sick, staying home from elementary school to hole up in bed with a cardboard box full of paper dolls. Her little kneecaps stood up to make silky white mountaintops for her dolls to traverse. When they fell, they lost limbs, amputations Mary doled out methodically with a pair of scissors from her art kit. This, she told herself, was their punishment. This was what they deserved for trying to escape the white-linen world she'd built for them. She was obsessed with justice and retribution, concepts that had boggled her mind since the 1950 arrest of Julius and Ethel Rosenberg, betrayers of America. Mary knew only a few details of the case — clips of information from the nightly news, snippets of conversation she overheard at cocktail hour. But she couldn't forget Ethel's unfocused gaze in the booking photos, published in the *Batavian,* or the reports that surfaced, following Ethel's 1953 execution, that after three shocks her heart still beat and smoke rose from the dry nest of her hair. It all seemed so horrific, so possible. A nightmare that could happen to anyone. The Rosenbergs had used a cut-up Jell-O box to commit their unforgivable crime. Mary had seen it, Imitation Raspberry held up to the courtroom by the U.S. attorney. What if he suspected her family, too? Just last month, her fourth-grade teacher had called her a Communist and sent her to the principal's office for repeating what Bob had said the night before: "This McCarthy guy's a hack."

After that, news of her alleged Communism had spread like wildfire throughout the school and persisted, even as a year passed and she graduated to the fifth grade. Tom was embarrassed by her. Mary herself felt haunted by a shame so deep it was animate, shaped like the specter of the Rosenbergs, like the gray-and-black figure of Joseph McCarthy, who had appeared on the television each night for years, his eyeglasses in one hand, his body hunched around a microphone.

The world shifted often in those days, characterized by falsities and false binaries. The bombers were coming but never came. Elfrida was considered less than, dumb and different, but was the kindest person in Mary's world, the only one who seemed to care. Tom was her brother, bound by blood but so cold that she sometimes imagined his contempt seeping through the walls of the house, snaking around drywall, wood, and stone. But the greatest pain came not from Tom but from two of his friends, who, in the weeks after her trouble at school, began to open Mary's bedroom door after she'd gone to bed.

She'd taken to sleeping in her dress-up clothes, falling into dream as Cleopatra one night, a gypsy queen the next. But when the boys arrived, they stripped away her layers, her imagined womanhood, touching and examining her with expressions of quiet concentration. When they left she was ashamed, unable to speak, to shout the way she wanted to. She'd learned what talking could do.

One night she awoke to the squeak of her

bedroom door. She kept her eyes closed, pretended to sleep, even as she felt a body enter the room, felt herself go rigid with expectation and dread. The boy climbed up on the side of her twin bed and slowly, trying not to wake her, reached his hands under the covers. She felt his fingers draw the hem of her nightgown carefully up her thighs. She kept her eyes squeezed shut. A floorboard squeaked in the hall, a pipe ticked in the ceiling above. The boy stopped moving. Mary opened her eyes, looked up at the shadow leaning over her.

"It's nothing," he said, almost comfortingly. "Be really quiet." She nodded. She had done this before. She knew to say nothing, to wait for him to finish, to ignore his fingers and the other soft and clammy parts of himself he placed in her hands, as if she would know what to do, as if her touch could unlock some purpose that seemed as much a mystery to him, Mary thought, as it felt to her.

The boy was seated beside her, touching her beneath the blanket, when Mary heard the footsteps. The boy didn't seem to notice. Not until the door swung open did he freeze. Mary curled into a tight ball, hiding her face in her hands, opening her fingers just enough to see Elfrida standing in the doorway, blocking the hallway light almost entirely, its glow making shapes out of the dips and curves of her silhouette. The boy slowly turned to look at her. "Get the hell out of here!" she screamed. "Get out!"

Elfrida told Midge what she'd seen, not quite sure what to expect. Midge loved Tom and Mary. But there was a reservation to her, a deep sense of decorum. She blushed easily at the bodily functions other mothers were inured to. And she avoided conflict, even with her own children. Elfrida probably wasn't surprised when, after that night, they never spoke of Mary and the boy again.

"Thank you, Elfrida" was all Midge said. "I'll handle it from here."

She climbed the stairs to bed, aware that her daughter's pain was now another burden for them both to carry. She tucked it up inside herself, resolving never to mention it again, not even to Bob. His temper ran hot, especially after so many bourbons, and she could imagine him confronting the boy, wrenching him from sleep, throwing him out the door. She could imagine having to explain the embarrassing details of Bob's anger to the boy's parents. But something had to be done.

Perhaps, Midge reasoned, leaving LeRoy

would solve Mary's problems. But boarding school seemed too painful a separation for her sensitive daughter, who was still so young. And wouldn't the whole family benefit from time away?

"The children should see the world," she said to Bob one morning, floating the idea of a year abroad. He agreed instantly, eager himself to leave LeRoy. What was all their wealth for, he boomed, if not for an adventure like this?

The plan developed quickly — a year in Europe as a family, a Volkswagen bus, a tutor — but the preparations were endless, maddening, and sometimes Midge wondered if they were worth it. But then she reminded herself of the weightlessness of travel, the world outside LeRoy; and the boys, little Mary prone in the dark.

She called friends and friends of friends, universities and boarding schools, looking for someone single but trustworthy to travel with them. Her search led to Mr. Ward Smith, soft voiced and cosmopolitan, who'd taught for years in Istanbul but lived now in New York. She hired him at once. She phoned Volkswagen and bought a bus they could pick up in Marseilles; she booked hotels in different cities and passage on an ocean liner. In October of 1957, she handed the keys to 141 East Main Street to the tweed-clad young couple who would be renting it, and the family left LeRoy.

Was the sea for Mary a balm? Stinging at first, but good, like salt poured in a wound to sterilize it, make it clean? Twelve years old now, she still dreamed of the boys and their black-magic shadows looming at her bedside. But as days passed on the ocean, her nightmares lessened. She rose each morning to walk the deck with her father, hinging her arm neatly into the crook of his elbow. They hung over the ship's railing, pointing out slivers of sunlight on the water or looking for the horizon, which disappeared into the ocean each morning, the two surfaces reflecting each other.

6

During the Second World War, when sugar was war-efforted into ration, Jell-O advertisements assured anxious cooks that the challenge was simply further incentive to make the Jell-O that *was* available even prettier. Pour it into the most elaborate molds! Bedizen it with the tastiest fruit and fixings! To help, General Foods produced promotions like *Bright Spots for Wartime Meals,* a 1944 Jell-O cookbook designed to advise those struggling under rationing. *Bright Spots* featured a new brand ambassador — another approximation of femininity based on a cartoonish outline of a woman's character. Plump and perky faced, housewife Victorianna is seen throughout the book pondering what to make. On one page she leans into her refrigerator, searching for solutions, clever tricks to disguise her lacking pantry. On the next she whips up miracles, presents them to a table full of guests. Her corpulent body presides over every meal, promising the bounty her country can't provide. But she never thinks about all that. She just lifts the dashed-off lines of her eyebrows, curls her shaded lips into a U. The dots of her eyes hang like pencil pokes, promising simplicity and stability, the sureness of order and routine. *Follow these simple steps,* she chirps, *and everything will be just fine!*

And what sweet victory when Victorianna was right! The steps worked, the war ended. America entered into a more prosperous economic state, and Victorianna's role shifted, changing with Jell-O's, which in turn became utterly dependent on the country's burgeoning domestic-science movement.

Fronted by women and born of the Industrial Revolution, the assembly line, and the space race, the domestic-science movement maintained that science and technology, when applied to housework and meal preparation, could simplify housekeeping, nourish families, and eradicate germs and sickness entirely. Previous generations of housekeepers (i.e., previous generations of *women*), as well as antiquated *European* practices such as sweeping and handwashing, were to blame for unkempt, disorderly

71

homes and the familial illnesses, addictions, and poverty they begot. In fact, all societal ills could be traced to the failings of women, and it was the job of modern wives and mothers to atone for the past, to streamline outdated housekeeping methodologies, to make a science of domestic labor.

Of primary importance was the control of food, which in its natural state was unclean and disorderly. And so it must be encapsulated, hidden in neat vessels, decorated to appear palatable. Jell-O, of course, was an imperative tool. But mayonnaise, for example, became another ingredient scientific cooks saw as indispensable. It was not uncommon to see chicken or tuna disguised by mayo, congealed with Jell-O, then shaped into the specter of the animal from which it originated. Consumers wanted the shadow of a thing, cleaner somehow in its transparency, but not the thing itself.

The more food could be processed and contained, domestic scientists reasoned, the easier it was to safely administer. A spoonful of sugar makes the medicine go down. Makes the medicine appealing, *familiar,* even, the further alienated it is from its original source: nature.

Even before industrialization pushed American housewives into the kitchen, salad preparation was considered the purview of the lady of the house, not a hired cook or maid. Plucking and carving could be left to the help. But only a lady could rein in and refine the fruits of the earth. Salads were enmeshed with nature, which was in turn enmeshed with femininity (a correlation often detrimental to women throughout the ages), and the addition of a salad course not only rounded out a meal but also feminized it. Light and decorative, clean and delicate — these were the attributes a salad, and a lady, should possess. The production of a salad too beautiful to eat was the epitome of success for modern domestic scientists and contributed to the widely circulated notion that women's appetites were as dainty as the salads and desserts they labored over. Anemic girls and women, green with chlorosis — a pallor considered beautiful — were the norm in the late 1800s, and although future generations of women consumed more meat, a bloodthirsty young lady was, and perhaps still is, considered unnatural.

Jell-O's light and dainty demeanor fit well with the dietary restrictions of girls and women in the 1800s and 1900s. Advertisements heralded its low caloric composition (calories also being a modern scientific revelation), and recipe books came equipped with charts outlining the correct serving sizes for Jell-O desserts, salads, pies, and so forth. In the wake of the Second World War, advertisements continued to market Jell-O as uniquely *American* but also uniquely healthy.

Gone were the days when the full-figured Victorianna was needed to comfort anxious Americans, who, confronted by their dark and empty pantries, feared scarcity and hunger. Now, America had more bounty than it knew what to do with, and the country turned to women's bodies to reflect the necessary restraint. So it wasn't long before Jell-O's low-cal reputation was bolstered by a new, sugar-free variety, D-Zerta. Made with saccharin, D-Zerta clocked in at ten calories per serving, one-eighth the amount in regular Jell-O. "It takes a lot of willpower to keep counting calories," bemoans a thin blonde in a TV ad spot. She sits in the foreground of a child's birthday party, watching glumly as a similarly slender brunette frosts a chocolate cake. "Yeah, I know," her companion commiserates. "But give up dessert? Not me! Not when I've got D-Zerta!" D-Zerta, she informs her friend, handing her a dessert cup full of trembling pink, is sugar-free and low-cal. "I can treat myself to D-Zerta whenever I want," she says, the kids milling frantically in the background, "and not feel guilty."

7

In Europe, Bob and Midge took the children everywhere with them. Gone were the evenings out alone. Everyone went to the nightclub. Everyone drank the red wine and danced shoulder to shoulder on the packed floor until two in the morning. In Paris and Pisa and Rome, the family took separate paths through cathedrals and ruins, intersecting with each other from time to time. Mr. Smith circulated, whispering his lessons to the children, remarking on buttresses and stained glass to Midge and Bob. He often found Mary alone, sitting in a quiet spot and drawing her view in the small leather notebook Midge had given her. She journaled in images, chronicled her memories in the details of people's faces, the patterns in the tiles; she imitated the sculptures and facades she saw, imagining someday she might make art herself, not knowing she already was. She sent letters home to her best friend, Marcia, the margins filled with sketches of dancing women with full skirts and cleavage, their dresses always colored in bright shades of orange or red or green. These women, unlike any Mary had seen before, took root in her mind. They seemed so confident in their bodies, their voices, which boomed in greeting or insult to the other women they passed, the leering men. They were peasants, but to Mary they seemed like priestesses, imbued with a power to speak that traced straight back to divinity.

At night Mary sat on the window ledge of her hotel room, watching the winter rain fall outside, formulating a future for herself in the image of the women she admired. She would be thirteen soon. Her body was changing, and she was hyperaware of its newness. Men stared. *"Che bella!"* they called from across the street, blowing her kisses even as she walked arm in arm with her mother. She didn't know what to do when this happened. She thought of the women and sensed she'd soon need their magic, a deep, feminine witchcraft. At night she sat up while Tom slept and looked at herself, her own soft reflection in the lamp-lit windowpane, like something newly pieced together, something that had been shattered, then saved.

One room over, alone in her bathroom, Midge ran her hands down her neck and along the soft slope of her breasts, tracing new lines, new skin loosened by a weight loss she couldn't explain.

The nightmare began in Rome. Midge stayed in bed, pleading exhaustion and a headache. "A trip to the doctor's wouldn't hurt," Bob said, and it was decided; the next morning, she went. "I'm feeling much better," she said when she returned. They were at dinner, everyone drinking red wine. "Mary, darling," Midge said, changing the subject, catching her daughter as she reached for the carafe, "how about a little shopping tomorrow?"

They ventured out the next morning. "A dress, certainly," Midge said, "but undergarments, too." She steered her daughter into a small lingerie shop. "It's time for a brassiere," she practically whispered, flushing a little red as she touched Mary's arm. She stood by and watched as a wrinkled Roman woman measured Mary's waist and bust, the latter of which grew, it seemed to Midge, daily. She wasn't surprised when Mary fit into a C-cup brassiere. How could she have waited so long for this?

At lunch in a small café, Midge picked at her insalata while Mary ate osso buco, a dish she relished. "The rarer the better," she always said when ordering, to which Bob guffawed and Midge cringed. Her daughter's appetite was cavernous. She wanted it all. The finest lamb chops, tenderloins dripping bloody juices. And why shouldn't she have it? Midge reasoned. She'd learn soon enough to curb her hunger, she thought, reaching across the table to touch Mary's hand.

"I've something to tell you," she said. "Remember the doctors I visited with?"

Mary nodded.

"They found a lump in my breast," Midge said. "It could be nothing," she rushed, "but the doctors say it may be why I've been feeling so poorly."

Mary looked into her mother's face. It did look paler. And Midge did look thinner than before.

"Will everything be all right?" Mary asked.

"Oh yes, of course, lambie!" Midge said, her tone suddenly brightening. "But we do need to see to it. I need to have an operation."

They would leave the next morning for Palermo, where there was a reputable clinic, she said. Mary stared at Midge. She wasn't sure how she was supposed to react, so she searched for clues in folds and creases, in the bloodlessness, of Midge's skin, the slight frown above her eyebrows. What had Cousin John said about the curse again? She racked her mind, wondering what loophole Midge might have fallen into. No, she was a woman and therefore exempt. So it couldn't be that serious, Mary figured.

"Your father will stay with me," Midge went on. "Mr. Smith will take you and Tom to Istanbul, Greece, Beirut, and Egypt, just as we had planned." Afterward, Midge and Bob would meet the children in Portugal, and they'd all board a luxury liner, the *Vulcania,* together. They'd all go home.

Home? Mary almost yelled. She couldn't go home. Home was where her voice was punished. Home was where the boys were. Midge squeezed her hand. "Yes, but trust me, lambie, everything is fine — I'm going to be just fine." But Mary was shocked, unable to understand what her mother's illness had to do with her, unable to understand who was being punished, and for what.

In a day, Midge was gone. Bob checked her into the clinic, only to wind up trolling the halls outside her room, carrying magazines rolled into tubes he hit against his thigh in nervous rhythms. Meanwhile, Mr. Smith took Mary and Tom on adventures. They rode the ferry to the Aeolian Islands, sea spray on their faces. They toured Agrigento, the Valley of the Temples, where crumbling columns and walls and roofs jutted from the landscape in jagged lines, like the aftermath of a battle, dismembered limbs scattered.

Mary and Tom bickered fiercely on these outings.

"I've been saying it for years," Tom said. "We've been too much for Mother. We did this, we made her sick." Mary always took the bait, and always lashed back. "Calm down," Tom would tell her, his voice flat, emotionless. "I'm simply telling you the truth. Your oversensitivity is extremely taxing to be around."

Tom was usually this way in their arguments, infuriatingly calm, and Mary felt trapped by trying to defend herself without showing emotion. It was impossible. She always came off as crazy. She began to think her brother was right. Maybe she was that kind of girl. Maybe she was the crazy kind.

On their third day in Sicily, Mr. Smith took

Mary and Tom to the Capuchin Catacombs. As they descended a slippery staircase lit by torches, the wet stink of mildew grew, filling Mary's head. She missed her mother with a sharp pain; she wanted to reach out and hold someone's hand to steady herself. But neither Mr. Smith nor Tom felt appropriate to turn to. She touched the wall, slick with slimy condensate, then continued down. Tom and Mr. Smith had already reached the bottom.

"Keep up, Mary!" Tom called.

When she came to the foot of the stairs, she found herself in a dank corridor, its walls filled with hanging bodies, open-mouthed and fully clothed, dried skin flaking from their bones. In the slackness of the skeletons' jaws, the emptiness of their eyes and the tortured claws of their hands, Mary saw herself, her family, Edith and Ernest at home in LeRoy, packed into the family crypt and turning to gelatinous dust. She thought of the curse. She thought of her mother. *So* this *is where we all end up,* she thought. The prospect tightened in her sternum. And yet she followed, last in line, looking at her brother's back, as the narrow path wound them deeper into the cata-combs. Mr. Smith was narrating the jour-ney, but Mary heard none of it. So when they entered a separate room and saw a porcelain-skinned, thin-lidded child, swaddled in gauzy white and wearing a dusty pink hair bow, asleep under glass, she caught her breath, as if realizing the promise of life eternal. "This," Mr. Smith said, "is Rosalia Lombardo." Mary and Tom gathered around. A small plaque hung below her casket. *Nata 1918, Morta 1920.* It was uncanny how perfectly preserved she was, little Rosalia. How close to life. Her body seemed to float, suspended, in the vacuumed air, a ripe peach encased, the daintiest Jell-O mold. Everything was sweet, pink, appetizing. Rosalia wanted for nothing, hungered for nothing. She was the ideal little girl, silent. She would never argue with her brother or make her mother sick. Mary bowed her head, suddenly guilty for wanting so much freedom. For the first time in her life, she issued a silent prayer. *If I die,* she prayed, *please let me stay behind like this, perfect.* At least in death, she wouldn't disappoint.

It was the early spring of 1958 when the family boarded the *Vulcania* and returned to New York. Midge was still recovering from her surgery, guarding the site of her mastectomy, ashamed of her flattened chest.

She felt helpless, floundering to keep her head above the surface of the morphine she needed to cover the pain. The pain, inescapable and constant, a leaden throb radiating across the scarred terrain of her chest, down into the pit of her armpit, the space from which doctors had scooped diseased lymph nodes, little lumps of betrayal that pumped cancer into the whole of her. She felt compressed, her body squeezed of everything it had left to give. Now, entirely empty, she was less a woman than a woman-shaped hole. Every day she strapped on the stuffed mastectomy bra she'd ordered from a special company in New York. Every day she performed womanhood and wellness. But the impossibility of a convincing performance exhausted her. In fact, everything exhausted her. Especially the children, who'd bickered increasingly since returning to LeRoy. Every evening their thin voices nattered through the floorboards, the walls, becoming the soundtrack to Midge's worsening pain. When it reached a crescendo, she packed a bag and checked into the hospital, this time Strong Memorial in Rochester, a hospital well funded by Woodward wealth.

The prognosis was initially good. The pain was simply the pain of healing tissue, doctors said. But, lying alone in her hospital bed each night, Midge battled the voice inside her, telling her they were wrong. She couldn't bear the thought of death, the unfairness of it. She thought of everything she hadn't done, everywhere she hadn't traveled. And of her children, too young to live motherless. Mary in particular was a source of concern. Who would usher her into womanhood? Who would teach her what to wear, what to say or not say; who would teach her what (or whom) to avoid? These questions spun in Midge's mind, spurred by pain and a frantic, grasping fear. To silence them she slept, falling into a darkness made dreamless by the morphine she asked for anytime the pain whispered, knowing it would soon shout, then scream, always bearing the same truth: she was dying.

The pain took its toll, as did the drugs. When Midge came home from the hospital, it was as a sliver of herself. It was as if her body were preparing to empty, a house packed with boxes, not yet vacated, but almost. She sat at the dinner table in her bathrobe, soft blue with pink rosebuds scattered over the fabric like the cherry blossoms that littered the front lawn each spring. She ate in tender bites, as if the inside of her mouth were sore. Afterward, seated in the living room, her feet on a small footstool, she stared at her swollen ankles, her purple toes with their lacquered red nails.

Midge's feet in particular disgusted Mary, who felt guilty for her repulsion, not knowing it was simply fear covered over. What had become of her mother's body, once soft and clean? Something evil, inherently bad, had changed Midge from the inside out. Mary began to avoid her, giving her a wide berth and swallowing her annoyance when Midge called to her from the sofa or bed, asking for water. Their relationship became one-sided. Consumed by her illness, unable to console her daughter, Midge became the needy one. She was always asking for something: water, towels, help to the bathroom, help back to bed. But when Mary asked her a question, she didn't answer, just stared at the floor, the wall, instead. *What's wrong with you?* Mary wanted to shout, but didn't. Her mother was sick. Her mother was recovering. Her mother would return, Bob promised; she just needed time. So Mary stayed away, holed up in her room, reading romance novels with fainting ingenues on their covers. When school began in August, ushering Mary into the eighth grade, she bore the bullies, older boys determined to put her in her place. She had wanted to fit in, wanted to be a *good girl* to match the closet full of dresses Midge had ordered her from Sibley's in Rochester in her last motherly act, each garment complacent, conforming. But LeRoy magnified Mary's difference, and she railed against its smallness. Each night at the dinner table, she complained about the narrow-mindedness of the kids at school. "And the teachers," she'd say, her voice rising, "they're no better — they encourage it!" Her pomposity was extreme. *She* had been to Europe, she reminded her friends constantly; *she* had seen things. And she had. Mary was ahead in all her classes. She spent the whole year fantasizing about returning to Europe just to revisit Rosalia. Distance — from the boys, from her constant surveillance — became her purest reprieve.

Soon, Mary began filling out boarding school applications with a determination she'd later describe as deluded. *Mother will be better soon,* she thought. And at a prep school, Mary imagined, she'd be suitably appreciated — praised, even — for her worldliness, a trait frowned upon in LeRoy. As it was, Midge, who usually stepped in to ground her daughter's self-importance, was silent. She was asleep most days when Mary and Tom returned from school and woke some nights only to ease herself to the dinner table, stare at her plate, then return to bed.

In years to come, Mary would think of the night as a threshold, a transformative doorway she passed through in order to know her mother's illness, to assume it. It was February, not late, but already dark. The moon was out, casting shadows on the snow, shapes Mary would later remember like specters, the looming bearers of bad news. Midge had been silent for days. She still moved about the house at mealtimes, but her eyes were newly glazed over, her expression permanently confused. Once seated, she required help to rise, and Tom and Bob stood on either side of her, lifting her upright by the elbows. She'd ask for an arm then, to make it to the bathroom, where she'd linger for an unnatural span of time, Bob knocking softly to ask if she was okay.

This was how it started, that February evening, the soft knock, the pleading question. But this time, Bob entered after he knocked. When he came out, he was paler and strode in a fog toward the living room.

At least this is how Mary remembered him, suddenly shocked by Midge's decline.

But perhaps it was she who was shocked. Of course Mary knew Midge was ill, but everyone kept saying she'd get better. And though her father seemed shaken when he walked from the bathroom, he must have already realized that Midge's cancer was too rooted to cut out. He must have been arguing with her for days, weeks, even, about returning to the hospital. But Midge knew what would happen if she did. She emerged from the bathroom on her own after Bob left, faltering as she tried to stand, her brow furrowed, her bathrobe hanging limply from her shrunken frame.

"Mary, darling," she said to her daughter, who was standing in the kitchen, flipping through a magazine. "Mary, the ambulance is coming to take me away."

Mary looked at her mother's face, her eyes at once wild and scared, changed by the morphine Mary didn't know she needed.

"Mom?" she said, rushing to her side, linking Midge's arm as if they might go for a stroll. "Mom? Why are they coming? What's wrong?" The doctors had continued to insist Midge was improving. Mary had chosen to believe them. But now she could hear her father in the living room, talking on the phone, his voice hushed and urgent. Something was not right. "One Forty-One East Main Street," he was telling the operator. "Please hurry."

"It's a mistake," Midge said, suddenly panicked, her tone mimicking her daughter's anxious alarm. "Your father doesn't know what he's doing — don't let him answer the door," she begged, tugging at Mary's sleeve. "Hide me. *Hide me!*"

Mary, unsure of what to do, put her hands on her mother's shoulders, then recoiled at their smallness, the nearness of her bone. "Sit right here," she said, propping Midge on a chair. "I'm going to go get help." There were sirens in the distance now, wailing closer. They were only blocks away. She looked around. Where could she hide her mother? The linen closet? The basement?

The ambulance was outside now. Midge was sitting, hands in her lap, rocking back and forth and gazing at the floor. "You have to hide me," she kept muttering. She seemed to have no other words. Mary heard the knock on the front door. She heard Bob's footsteps in the foyer, heard him open the door. She was panicking now. "Wait here, Mommy," she said. "I'll protect you." But, frantic and confused, she did something that would haunt her for the rest of her life. Not knowing why, she bolted out the back door and into the cold.

The immediate slap of the frigid air on her face felt good. The wet sting of snow inside her slippers gave her something to focus on as she crouched, a criminal, behind the toolshed, watching the red and blue ambulance lights bounce off the icy ground, turning the backyard into a stained-glass scene, a world of color. Into this world Mary placed herself as she waited for the ambulance doors to slam, the siren to wail again, loud at first, then diminishing.

8

Mary would have imagined her mother's death, her own grief, in the grandiose terms of the novels she read. She would have pictured herself fainting, collapsing in a pale heap of bedclothes. She would have imagined herself inconsolable, sobbing violently for days. She would have imagined her appetite waning, sleep evading her. She would have imagined all this if she had known to. But in actuality, she hadn't understood that Midge could truly die until she did. And even then, after the initial shock, nothing really changed. At least it seemed that way.

After the ambulance came for her, after her attempt to escape it, Midge had stayed in the hospital for good. Bob was protective of her — or perhaps he was protecting the children; Mary couldn't quite tell. Either way, he never let them visit, returning home with bloodshot eyes to answer their questions with assurances of *Soon, soon.*

It was a late night in April when the phone rang. Mary heard it from bed and put down the book she was reading, climbed from beneath the covers, and came to the top of the stairs in her nightgown. Recently, she'd been admitted to Kent Place School, a boarding school for girls in Summit, New Jersey, and it was all she could think of. Would the other girls be better read? She spent most of her time tearing through the canon, imagining as she read how free she'd feel once she left LeRoy. She imagined herself an intellectual, debating with her classmates, bookish girls in glasses. She imagined she might bond with these girls, become sisters. She rarely thought about her mother. Midge's death seemed impossible until it happened.

She found Tom in the foyer that April night sitting at their mother's desk, the receiver wedged between his shoulder and ear. She watched him as he scribbled notes, saying only *uh-huh.* When he hung up, he looked at his sister, holding the banister. He wore a stunned expression. "That was Dad," he said numbly. "Mom just died. I have a list of people here to call."

In the days after her mother's death, Mary

found that instead of falling apart, she became obsessively detail oriented. She was efficient. She slept deeply each night and ate when meals were served. She preoccupied herself with what to wear to Midge's funeral. She worried about Bob. She did not think of the day she and Midge shopped in Rome, or the day Midge was loaded into the ambulance and taken; she did not think about her mother's last words to her — *Hide me!* — and she did not think about the days and months and years to come. She was present, perfect, shocked into silence and her new role as a motherless daughter.

On the morning of the funeral, Mary fastened one of her Roman brassieres and stepped into a white silk slip. She craned her arm to zip the emerald dress her mother had bought her. She was suddenly older, more beautiful, her dark hair newly cut to a short bob, so that the curls curved gracefully around the soft lines of her face. "A young Elizabeth Taylor," people often told her, and she glowed in reply, her body a gemstone, absorbing praise like sunlight, hot to the touch. But today the knowledge of her beauty disappeared into silence, into the absence of her mother's voice. Everything was muted. Everything was dull: the fabric of her dress, once rich and deep, the floral-patterned wallpaper outside her room, the array of colorful clothing in her closet. And the creamy powder on Midge's armoire, one shade too light for her when she had puffed it over her face that morning, unsure of how to do so, mimicking her mother. "Mary Edith, you're so pale," people said to her at the reception, admiringly but concerned, and Mary thought to herself it was only the powder. She thought she'd fooled them. She thought to herself how unfeeling she was, floating above her life, her mother's death, like the film at the top of a drink not yet shaken.

Two years before, in Europe, they'd passed a mourning party. Women in black shawls, rending their hair, hysterical in their grief. Midge had taken Mary's hand and shuffled them along, eyes averted. But Mary had secretly turned to steal one more look. The women convulsed as they screamed and sobbed, exorcising the demon of their sadness. What freedom, Mary thought now, to feel so much, to love so deeply. Everything here was felt in secret, so she wasn't sure if she felt anything at all. How would it be different if she were allowed to be hysterical about her mother's death? What were the circumstances that would warrant such behavior? She knew those European women were expected to bear certain hardships without complaint. She knew that even as they wailed and howled, they were performing, artificially at times. The performance itself was a requirement of their sex. But wasn't there still truth to it? In Europe, death was everywhere acknowledged, a question posed by each little candle lit at each cathedral, by the artwork and sculpture, the crucifixes, catacombs, and cemeteries. Not like here, Mary thought, not like in LeRoy, where the realness of her loss was tucked away, silenced by superficial assurances that her mother was in a better place, consolations like the sugary toppings and layers of mayonnaise on the Jell-O molds guests carried with them when they entered the house, offerings of perfect sweetness to Midge's memory. Mary was fourteen now, nearly a woman. It was her job to accept these offerings, to smile and nod and assure the world she would manage her emotion, contain it inside her, a spell in a bottle, and shelve it away.

Drinking helped. Everything about Midge's funeral was punctuated by the glug of upended bottles. By nine a.m., Bob was chugging rye from a bottle stashed in the pantry; by ten, John had arrived and joined him. When the family left the house and headed to the funeral, the men reeked of it, caustic and tart.

"Religion is for nutjobs," Bob liked to say, but he cowed in the end to propriety. A generic service, fine. Mary sat next to him on the hard wooden pew, focusing on the only stained-glass window, a phoenix on a bed of fiery ashes, its wings half-spread, its talons uncurling. The bird was supposed to be hopeful, a symbol of rebirth. But Mary felt cheated by its false promise. She didn't cry. But she must have worn an angry look because after the service she was pulled into the pantry just the same.

"Here," said Cousin John, craning his elbow around her shoulders, his forearm pressing into the back of her neck, "drink this."

She took a short swig from the bottle. The bourbon burned going down. "Not yet," she said when John started to screw the cap back on. She took a glass from the shelf and held it out to him.

They stayed there, in the pantry, for another glass, then another, hiding out, watching the caterers carry trays in and out of the dining room, the swinging door between kitchen and crowd clapping closed, and open again.

Mary awoke in the late afternoon to the sound of the last guests still milling about downstairs, pots and pans clattering in the kitchen. Her cousin Joan was sitting in the armchair by the window, smoking a cigarette, which glowed with each drag she took. *An angel's heart,* Mary thought as Joan stubbed it out. "You're awake," she said. "Welcome back."

Joan had always been distant, quiet at dinner parties and during holidays — if she showed up at all. But now she spoke to Mary with a soft familiarity, as if sickness and loss made her relatable. "If you need to throw up, you should," she said, lifting the metal wastebin from its station beneath Mary's bedside table and placing it at her feet. "It'll make you feel better." Joan smiled.

Mary smiled back shyly, not sure if she could accept Joan's help, not sure what she had to offer in return. It seemed Joan wanted nothing. She camped out at the house on East Main Street for days, doting on Mary in particular, waiting for her to return from school each afternoon, wrapping her arms around her in the night as she fell into heavy, dreamless sleep. "You should get out of here," Joan said one morning, seated by the window in her nightgown, dragging on her cigarette. "Go to Europe for school, why don't you? Find work you like, depend on yourself. Don't stay in LeRoy. And don't," she added, stubbing her smoke into an ashtray, "drink so much. Trust me," she said. "It never turns out well."

After Midge's death, time sped up, a blur of days and nights beginning and ending. Joan left abruptly one afternoon while Mary was at school. The next morning another cousin, Betty, cleaned out Midge's closets, scooping nylon stockings into bags, sweeping bottles of nail polish into shoe boxes. She left only Midge's bathrobe, her jewelry, and her ivory-handled hairbrush with irises carved into its hilt. Bob seemed to like it better this way, absent any reminders of his wife. He began making the cocktail-party circuit, taking Mary along as a date. She, in turn, asked to invite John.

The parties were always the same. Someone's living room, someone's bar cart, no one speaking Midge's name, Bob drinking bourbon after bourbon, leaning on Mary as she helped him back to the car — John suddenly nowhere to be found — then driving him home. It was as if her mother had been erased. It was as if Mary were entirely alone. *Well,* she thought, *if this is how it has to be now, I might as well embrace it.* She imagined boarding school, a new life as a new girl, as she squinted at the road, seesawing the wheel to stay straight.

Even though John was prone to disappearing, he made the parties bearable. When his attention was turned on her, Mary felt the world melt away. When he was distracted, roped into a conversation, or dancing with one of his many admirers, there was always a drink to be had. They went hand in hand, Mary's handsome cousin and the gin and tonics she had begun to crave around four each afternoon. She held her glass in one hand as John twirled her, sometimes even pressing his nose into her neck when he thought nobody was watching.

"He's making a fool of you," Tom said. But Mary only shrugged.

"I'll be gone in September anyway," she said. She couldn't wait to pack her things and leave.

9

Thanksgiving that year, the first without Midge, was served at John and Jessie's house in Rochester. John sat next to Mary for the whole cocktail hour, elbows on his knees, a squat glass of bourbon cradled in his hands, asking her about boarding school. "Your mother would be proud," he said when she struggled to answer, his hand on her forearm, his eyes not wavering from hers.

It had been a six-hour train ride from Kent Place School back to LeRoy, and Mary's body buzzed with pent-up energy. Even at school she felt this way, trapped. Her room was small, puritanical in its whiteness. She was one of forty boarding students and one of only seven freshmen; most of the students commuted from home. This might have created a close community, she'd thought, but for most of her first semester at Kent Place, she'd found herself alone, mechanically following rules and routines she wasn't subject to at home. Set mealtimes and bedtimes, curfews, a strict visitation policy that prevented boarders from leaving campus.

So Mary had to search for something to tell John about Kent Place. There was little she could tell him that wasn't deeply private, somehow indecent to reveal. She'd taken Midge's ivory hairbrush from home, and it was her most important possession besides her books. After lights-out, wrapped in her quilt, she secreted novels and contraband cartons of crackers into the bathroom. She padded the bathtub and made a nest there. She preferred books to sleep. In books, she forgot about herself, her mother, whom she encountered in dreams, transformed into a vampire, a witch, hungry for her own daughter's blood. In class, she argued with her teachers, disputing their claims about places in Europe she'd already been, novels she'd already read. She simmered in her own rising rage and was called impertinent and rude. In etiquette class, she was told to slow down and, for heaven's sake, to keep her mouth closed. Her only escape was literature. She favored the classics, burning through all of Dickens and the Brontës in her first year. She loved the weight of the books in her lap, the thin pages painting her stories of poverty and romance and the Gothic occult, its crosses to bear and crises of faith.

So what could she tell Cousin John? The truth was that Mary wanted to be wanted, irresistible, a heroine. She wanted to be seen. And now, sitting in front of him, his attention burning into her, she thought of how often, on those lonely nights in the boarding school bathtub, she'd fantasized about him.

No one at Kent Place knew about her mother. If they did, it was an afterthought, something they expected her to process and be done with. There is an expiration date on sadness, she'd learned. There is an expectation that one must move on, get over it, accentuate the positive. The passion and pain and periods of mourning in the novels she read were a fiction; they weren't allowed in her world. Except with John. With him she felt justified in her grief, how it made her want to rend her garments, to rage. He seemed to understand this impulse.

"Mary." Jessie's voice punctured her thoughts. John's hand flew from Mary's arm, recoiling instinctively. "Would you gather up the drink orders?"

"Of course," Mary said, seething on the inside. She rose, smoothing her skirt and walking around the room asking, "May I get you a drink?" the way Midge taught her, then retreating to the pantry to fill the orders. In the glass doors of the liquor cabinet, she looked at her own sallow face. It was a sad face, she thought. It was the face of someone alone in the world. But the next moment, John's reflection joined hers in the glass pane. And then his hands were on her shoulders, turning her around to face him. And then his lips were on her lips, erasing every other feeling. And then there was only the brush of skin, the ache of it.

Back at Kent Place, she reclined, resplendent on her bed, surrounded by her dorm sisters, regaling them with stories of her dashing cousin John. They put their hands over their mouths when she detailed how he'd kissed her, hard and wet and wanting.

Suddenly she was popular. Suddenly the other girls on the floor wanted her counsel and friendship. In the months that followed, they started calling her Mother Mary for the way she held court on her bed, inviting them to her inner sanctum to hear tales of her exploits with John, to confess their troubles and receive her advice. She nurtured them, giving — and receiving — the attention she craved herself. It was only natural that sometimes she scandalized them. But so what? She hoped she did. She meant to be motherly *and* bad. Honest with the girls the way Midge never was with her. She chain-smoked and said *hell* and *damn,* later adding *shit* and *fuck* with abandon. She signed the logbook, saying she'd be staying with a day student who lived just down the street, but really she was on the train to New York, sandwiched in between two other *bad girls,* whispering dirty jokes, cracking into laughter that made the other passengers, the men in suits and the women in their pillbox hats, turn around and stare. In the city, the girls walked Fifth Avenue, holding their purses with white-gloved hands. They mimed the postures of the mannequins in the windows at Bendel's and Saks. It was 1961, the era of circle skirts and wide shawl collars, silk turbans and furs, items the girls coveted as talismans of the womanhood they were entering into. Sometimes, inside the gilded gold doors, they had their makeup done, sitting like dolls for the powder-faced women who plucked and puffed and primped them to perfection. Sometimes Mary bought rouge or lipstick, sometimes a sweater, something functional and warm for the cold New Jersey winter. Sometimes, though, she slipped a folded scarf into her handbag, sometimes an extra set of gloves.

The girls called themselves the Klepto Club. For the most part, they perpetrated their crimes in Summit, celebrating their hauls at the local soda fountain after a successful steal. But then word got out that someone had snitched, that the headmistress was hot on their trail, and Mary knelt over the toilet, unraveling her one big take, a navy-blue cashmere sweater, the soft strands of which she flushed away.

After that she changed her ways. The only thing worse than staying at Kent Place was getting kicked out. Especially now that a new girl had arrived on her floor. Judy was from Alaska. Small and blond, but tough, she wore her outsider identity unmistakably, like a scratchy tag sticking from the collar of her dress. Mary couldn't stop staring at her. When Judy looked back, it was with an expression of anger and then recognition.

Late at night the two girls sat cross-legged on Mary's bedroom floor, wrapped in their quilts, a flashlight in the circle's center, while Judy pried the lid off a can of smoked Portlock salmon, sent all the way from a place called Squeaky Anderson's in Cordova, Alaska. She was full of stories: family fishing dates and grizzly bear attacks. The only thing she rarely spoke of was her mother, dead of cancer, just like Midge. Mary never pushed it — what was there to say? She knew what it felt like inside the mind of a motherless girl. Long stretches of icy numbness inside and then rage, fear, and a dull longing for something she knew she could never have.

Sometimes on weekends or vacations, the girls went to LeRoy or visited Judy's grandmother, a wealthy old woman with a house in Summit. Sometimes they drew apart and Mary took the train home alone, returning each time to a town unchanged by her absence, her mother's absence. There were the same red and yellow leaves, the same neat piles of them on the lawn outside each house; the same kids hanging out at the soda fountain on Main Street, ringing the jingle bells hung on the door each time they entered or left. The same pillows on her bed, the same dolls on the shelf. It made sense, then, that she half expected to find Midge at her writing desk, licking envelopes, signing her name in that delicate draw of ink so unique to her.

There were some small changes, of course. The absence of a photograph that made Bob weep, the presence of empty Scotch bottles stacked beside the trash bin. Without Mary in the house, Bob and Tom had let Elfrida go. "No!" Mary cried when Tom told her nonchalantly the afternoon he picked her up for a long weekend home. "How could you?" she demanded, her voice growing higher, thinner, threatening to shout. "Why didn't you think to ask me?" Tom shrugged and said nothing. He was getting taller now, although not by much. In the wide-openness of his face, Mary thought she'd seen a lessening of something, the sibling rivalry they'd carried on for years, maybe. But now he seemed unfeeling again. She stared at him, wishing her eyes could bore holes into his face, to get at the feeling beneath the wooden mask he'd assumed.

"Well," he said, "I guess she was sick." He kept his eyes on the road. "I actually think she might have died."

Mary lost her breath as her anger turned to shock, her whole body dropping suddenly downward, as if swept through a trapdoor, out of the car, out of LeRoy, into a blackness where she floated, fluid and afraid.

"That's right," he said. "I'm remembering now, she died."

For a long moment Mary was silent, her face blank and seized up, as if possessed. But she shook herself back to the car and her brother's impassive expression, which filled her with a feral urge to strike him. Instead she struck herself, pounding her fists hard into her thighs and repeating, "Why the hell didn't someone let me know?" as she sobbed, releasing everything she'd tucked tightly into the box behind her solar plexus, the same place she hid all the feelings she'd learned were unutterable.

"Jesus Christ, Mary," Tom said, glancing over at her as if she were deranged. "We didn't want to bother you."

She was crying in loud, violent gasps, but by the time they arrived home, she was calm again, everything siphoned back into the box where it was hidden, safe. Mourning was a luxury she couldn't afford. To dwell on her loss, her anger, her fear of death, would only drive her mad, she told herself as she climbed from the car, grabbed her suitcase from the trunk. But she couldn't help but think of the Jell-O curse Cousin John had warned her of. It was the men who were vulnerable, he'd said. But Mary was beginning to suspect it was the other way around.

■ ■ ■ ■

She spent the afternoon in her room until Tom's voice called through the door. "Stop sulking," he said. "John's here."

"Shit shit shit," she muttered as she dug through her suitcase, looking for her best dress, the dark-blue one with the tight waist, the tapered skirt. When she found it, she pulled the hem to loosen the wrinkles. "Oh well," she said to no one as she stepped into it, contorting her arms to work the zipper. She'd seen John once since the kiss, and he hadn't repeated it. But she wished he would with a longing that felt like sorrow and joy compressed into a single, smarting bruise, pulsing to be pressed. In the bathroom she patted her hair with water and Royal Crown hair cream, the only thing that even began to keep her dry curls looking combed out and straight. She dug a pill bottle from her ditty bag and shook two Dexedrines into her palm.

The Dex had come from the mother of a day student, who had given them to Mary, along with a random array of other diet pills. "I can easily get more," the mother had said, handing her several bottles and winking. "A girl's got to keep her figure — better to be looked over than overlooked." The mother, it seemed, felt that Mary's best investment was to sculpt the outlines of her body. Mary had potential, so she shouldn't waste it: diets and trim figures were regimens to be maintained no matter what.

With the pills, Mary had shed pounds like they were a second skin, a buffer between her body and the world. She hungered for nothing and wanted for nothing. Her breath was shallow, her heartbeat quick. Her hands shook. She stayed up late reading, avoiding sleep and nightmares of her mother. In class she tapped her pencil manically on her desk. Suddenly other girls envied her body, which had shrunk around the waist and face, giving her the hourglass figure of a movie star in only a month's time. *You're so tiny,* the girls pouted, putting their hands on her waist, then doing the same to themselves, comparing. Men stared more than ever now. They called to her from cars when she walked into Summit on the weekends. *Hey, baby, hey, sweetie, hey, sexy.* But now that she was home in LeRoy, no one seemed to notice. Not Tom and certainly not Bob, who had looked at her when she came in from the car with the same glazed-over eyes he turned on everything since Midge's death.

That evening, after she swallowed the pills in her room, she slipped into short navy pumps and walked downstairs and into the parlor. Cousin John saw her and stood immediately. "My God, Mona," he said, running his eyes down her. In his expression Mary recognized something about her body, something strong about it, when molded to fit a man's desires.

John came back the next morning to take her to the shooting range. He waited in the car, watching her as she shut the front door behind her and walked toward him, wearing tight, tapered trousers and a fitted button-down blouse that showed off her waist. She slid into the passenger side of his Mercedes, and he leaned over, his lips next to her ear. "You look beautiful," he whispered. She smiled. The power she felt, the control she suddenly had over her body, over John, pushed through her, *elation.* On the way, as the car snaked over dips and rises in the road, John reached over and put his hand on her thigh. She said nothing, just collected the thrill of his touch, his desire, which felt like something dropping inside her, an excited thread from the base of her sternum to her lowest point, that place Midge had called her modesty.

At the range, he stood behind her, his arms wrapped around her arms, even though she was already an excellent shot. He pretended to teach. "Hold it more like this," he said. When she called *pull* and the clay pigeon released, the gun kicked back into both of them, the crack of the shot reverberating in their ears.

Afterward they had lunch at the country club, and then John drove the car to a quiet strip of road and pulled over. The car fell silent but for the occasional whir of a passing automobile. After some time he spoke.

"Let me see you," he said, not saying her name, not calling her Mona.

"What do you mean?" She turned in her seat to face him.

He reached over, unbuttoned the top two buttons of her blouse. When he finally kissed her, it felt violent. But he wanted her; it was because he wanted her so badly. He told her so. "Just you wait, Mona," he said, squeezing her leg and clawing the flesh. She felt something like heat inside her, radiating from the V of her legs where his hand was inching, closer, closer. The place the boys had entered when she was only eleven, their intrusion an erasure of the girl she'd thought she was. Good, obedient. An inoffensive girl, always offering. A Jell-O girl, the Rockwell vision. What a lie. Striving for that had gotten her nowhere. It had certainly gotten Midge nowhere. Even so, Mary had tried, briefly. The funeral, the reassurances she'd offered. The real feelings they replaced had broken from the box and gathered now, excessive, beneath her skin. She wanted to release them. She wanted violence, sex. The two felt inextricable. Embodiment. In the shadow of her mother's death, she wanted to *live,* to remake herself in the image of the European women she'd drawn in her journals, their unrestrained breasts unapologetic, their thick thighs swinging from the slits of their skirts, their faces every variation of strange beauty, sneering and smiling at the men who jeered and catcalled. These women smelled of pungent body odor, not the sweet talcum and perfume her mother had used to hide herself in a cloud of artificial scent. They snapped the necks of birds and boiled the bones with sausage and spice, stirring the pot like witches. They ate with abandon. They *mourned.* This was who she wanted to be, this was who she could be with John. If only he would have her. "Not here, not here," he kept repeating, fending her off. But his hand still gripped her leg, moving now of its own accord to straddle him. He was breathless when he gently steered her from his lap, kissing her forehead, then breathing in her ear, whispering, "Soon, soon," as if soothing the child inside her.

10

For every American woman with household responsibilities, awareness of a meal's order, its organization, was considered essential by domestic scientists. To this end, recipe booklets had long been a staple of Jell-O's marketing campaigns. But in 1961, when my mother was sixteen, the small-booklet form was replaced with a ninety-five-page cookbook containing more than 250 recipes. *Joys of Jell-O* and its numerous sequels are still in use, available on eBay for five bucks, in fact: a steal, given that in the early 1960s, the cookbook sold for twenty-five cents plus proof of purchase of six Jell-O cartons, a sum equivalent today to around seven dollars.

Pricey, but worth it. Among the revolutionary recipes contained in its pages are five different variations on Jell-O Bavarian cream, the saucily titled Jell-O Hawaiian Eyeful, a mix of celery, pineapple gelatin, and fruit, and a Jell-O glaze for ham, sweet potatoes, and roast duck. Each recipe in *Joys of Jell-O* is summarized by a brief sentence beneath its name, explaining the occasion for which this particular Jell-O mold is best suited. The ladyfinger dessert, for example, is *for special occasions* and should be molded into the shape of a *flag, heart, bell or other symbol* in accordance with the closest holiday. The more modest cardinal-pear mold is simply *an easy way to glamorize inexpensive canned pear halves.* The Waldorf mold is a *lovely luncheon entrée* when served with cold cuts and hot muffins. The rhubarb salad, however, should be presented as *a tangy crisp contrast* to a more robust meat course. Ditto the minted pineapple, and cucumber cream.

Although most *Joys of Jell-O* recipes are carefully cordoned into their own category — dessert or salad — the slim and edgy "Two Way" chapter presents recipes that *defy someone to say that you're not ready for anything.* These molds may be (daringly!) served as either desserts or salads, so long as their category is made *absolutely* clear. It is the critical responsibility of the lady of the house to alert guests to the role a specific mold plays in the order of the meal. Desserts should *consistently* be garnished with prepared sweet toppings or whipped cream; salads *must* be unmolded on crisp greens and topped with dressing and mayonnaise.

At the end of the day, housewives were responsible for strengthening and maintaining the nuclear American family. It therefore made perfect sense that gathering everyone for set mealtimes three times per day ensured not only that they would eat, grow strong, and flourish — but also that they would absorb the strong *American* values the country's future depended on. It was important that Father sit at the head of the table, dispensing wisdom; it was imperative that Mother serve healthy, well-balanced meals. Mental and physical nutrition must be tended to. And Jell-O was here to help, to nourish and cajole, to serve as the centerpiece of social order.

Never in my mother's childhood had breakfast or lunch been particularly privileged. Bob was usually gone when the rest of the house awoke and Midge and the children ate Cream of Wheat in the kitchen, sometimes eggs and bacon on Sundays or on the first day of school. Come dinnertime, Midge and Bob *tried* to sit down at the table with their children. And sometimes they succeeded, Midge positioned at one end of the polished dining table, Bob at the other, while Elfrida swept in and out of the swinging door to the kitchen bearing lamb or pot roast, hot buttered rolls and potatoes. Sometimes, though, dinnertime came and went, and Elfrida, tired of listening to the hungry children whine, sat them down in the kitchen and served them chicken and Minute Rice and stewed buttery greens, all of them waiting for Midge and Bob to return from cocktails at Edith's mansion or listening to the laughter of the adult party going on in the parlor.

Now, without Midge, the group of cousins and friends that used to gather nightly in the East Main Street parlor had vanished. Bob was often out, mooching off someone's bar cart and ignoring mealtimes altogether. His absence frightened Mary. His grief, which he wore on his winnowed body, engulfed her own. She had wanted to be nurtured through the loss of her mother. She had wanted to act out her sadness, to try on identities — *bad girl, Mother Mary, Mona* — and find the one that would suit her best in this new, motherless world. But she'd quickly realized that she would have to put all that aside if she wanted to keep her father from falling apart. She would have to give to him all the nurturing she wanted for herself. The only way she could think to do so was to feed him. So on the weekends Mary came home from school, and every night during summer vacation, she tried to establish a seven o'clock dinnertime. In the kitchen, she'd flip timidly through Elfrida's old cookbooks. But she was unsure of what she could possibly master on her own. Without a woman to pass down recipes and techniques, Mary had little idea of what to make or how, and she tried too much too soon. Her Salisbury steak came out dry, oversauced, and rimmed in vegetables boiled gray; her roast chicken was too pink on the inside. But she kept trying. She had to. Her father was wasting away, and somehow she knew it was her duty to save him. It was what a woman did. If she could just assume the proper role, Mary thought, if she could nurture him like a woman, a wife, or maybe a mother, perhaps he would right himself, become the father whose wisdom could order the world. She longed for the day she could cease to be a centerpiece, the hub to which the spokes of her family attached. But this was her function now, a function Midge had escaped only in death. This was every woman's function: to be the piece that held the family, the culture, the country, together.

11

By 1963, Mary was a freshman at Sarah Lawrence College. She'd graduated from Kent Place in the spring, posing with Judy in matching white dresses and gloves, identical bouquets cradled in the crooks of their arms. Now she wore paint-splattered blue jeans and went braless under loose tops. She took the train into the city and spent afternoons at the Guggenheim, the Modern, the Met. She stood in front of Pollock's massive canvases and Nevelson's boxlike sculptures and imagined herself an artist. She pictured herself working in the city, teaching at Barnard, walking down Broadway, her portfolio in hand. While her father's self-negligence still constrained her at home, at least she was free of the rules that had ordered her life at boarding school. No more set meal- and bedtimes, no more classes on comportment. She saw it all for what it was, conformity, designed to keep people in their place.

In the city, in college, she felt freshly awakened, the way she had in Europe as a child. Art pulsed from New York, dangerous and alive. West of Fourteenth Street, Andy Warhol threw his parties. Dylan played in Greenwich Village. Patti Smith moved into the Chelsea Hotel. And Cousin John called twice a week.

Mary received his calls on her twin-sized dorm bed, where she would lounge, the telephone cord curled around her finger. Finally, John told her, now that he had her on her own — finally he could truly take her. "I want to make you mine, Mona," he whispered into his end of the line. "When can I see you?"

Mary giggled. "You tell me," she said, girlish and gamey, her voice babyish and soft. With him she was different from the self-assured woman she became when she wrote and spoke about art. Even art-making itself had begun to feel possible, and the idea of a life built around art and travel and adventure thrilled her, though she never mentioned this to John.

There was a freedom for her in the artist's way, a new way of managing the memories she'd tried so hard to shut off: her mother's body as it died, draining of life slowly, like a wilting plant, her desperate plea, *Hide me,* and Mary's cowardice, the slivers of siren and light glinting off the snow as she hid behind the shed. For years she'd worked to block these images, which came like flashes and infected her dreams. But in art, she could tap them, make something of them. Her professors praised the pieces she produced, painted and sculpted translations of her nightmares, which had only gotten worse with each year that Midge stayed dead. Her drinking, too, had worsened, and Mary woke most mornings unable to remember the night before. This, she told herself, was what she needed to create. She made a private mold for herself: isolated and addictive, the orphan-artist, tortured by visions of death. At night, barefooted and drunk on cocktails of bourbon and Dex, she strapped the welder's helmet to her head and drew the mask down over her face like a shell. In her hands fire and steel shaped predators — spiders and bony witch fingers, born of an endless loop between her unconscious world and her art.

"Meet me for dinner," John commanded. It was early November, a hint of winter on the air. He was coming into the city and staying at the Plaza. "I want you to see the Oak Room," he said, and Mary agreed coolly, but then hung up the phone and ran down the hall of her dorm, calling out to the other girls: "Who wants to go shopping!" She borrowed a green suede jacket and bought a new black sheath dress at Saks, a pair of velvet pumps that pinched her feet and made her teeter but looked, the salesman said, *as if they were stitched to your foot*, their arches fine, like those in the Notre-Dame Cathedral.

At the Plaza, in the dark-walled room, John ordered champagne that came nestled into a gold ice bucket. Light catapulted from the room's gilded accents into the bucket, piercing the bottle, and back out again. There was caviar and steak and a crème brûlée, the surface of which Mary daintily broke, chipping through the crusty top with the edge of her spoon, aware of John's gaze and how he watched her every move. "I like the way you do that," he'd say when she took a bite, as if everything about her were on display, presented like dinner for his consumption.

Afterward, after John signed the check and drank the last of his bourbon, he steered her toward the elevator, his hand on the small of her back. Mary felt herself moved into the gold box, a marionette in its theater.

There they stood side by side, nearly touching, and she could see her own misty body next to John's, reflected in the plated doors. When the doors opened, offering a threshold, Mary walked forward, teetering in her too-high heels.

In the bedroom John poured two bourbons. He loosened his tie, watched her fold her coat and slowly lay it over a chair. "Let's hurry, Mona," he said, throwing his tie on the bed, reaching for his glass. Mary wasn't sure what he meant by this. *What specifically does he mean for me to do?* She struggled to reach her zipper, moving slowly, stalling. She stepped from her dress carefully. "Now the rest," John said, still watching. Her face flushed. She shimmied out of her slip and stood before him in her underwear. She hadn't expected this. What she had expected, she didn't know. But not this. He sat down to remove his shoes and socks.
"On the bed," he demanded.
He left the lamp on. He had her sit on top of him, minus her brassiere, whose tight wires and bands she yearned for as soon as John removed them, exposing her to the light. He placed his hands on her hips and pushed into her in one swift motion, a shattering pain above which she hovered, ob-

serving herself from the ceiling while her cousin rocked her hips back and forth, agitating her body like an undeveloped photograph. From above, Mary saw the embarrassment of her breasts, ebbing and flowing with the rhythm of John's hands. She saw his face fold into a frown that deepened as the rhythm quickened, giving way to relief as his fingers squeezed tightly, leaving behind the indents of his nails, little crescents in her skin.

He slept after that. And Mary watched shadows, suspended on the ceiling, where she too had drifted, silent and disembodied. She felt full of food, sick with it, stuffed like a ballotine with everything she couldn't say. Once she'd thought she could confess to John and be understood; now she knew she had been wrong. She shouldn't have come here. She wanted to leave, but willing herself to rise felt impossible. Her whole body tingled, and she wondered if she could even move it. When John awoke and hastily dressed, pulling on his pants and saying *It's about time we get you home,* she pried herself off the bed, hiding her nakedness with a sheet, wavering on trembling legs when she stood. She moved about in a daze, gathering her clothes. When she found her slip, she stepped back into it, then did the same with her dress. But when she tried to catch the zipper, she realized she couldn't. Her right hand was frozen, clutched into a replica of her own sculpture, her fingers transformed into the claw of a crone, a witch. It stayed that way even after she asked John for help, suddenly mortified by having to do so; even after he packed her into a cab and handed the driver a ten-dollar bill; even after she returned to her dorm and retreated to the shower and scrubbed.

That night she did everything she could to cleanse herself, running the water so hot, it singed her skin, leaning over the toilet, trying to empty herself. When that didn't work, she sat on it instead. But no matter what she did, she couldn't unburden herself of the suffocating fullness she'd embodied since sleeping with John, since courting the curse, the meaning of which felt even foggier now. Once John had told her that the curse was out to get him, and *he* was the one in danger. But since he'd been inside her, Mary herself had literally frozen, her body like land torn up by excavation, then left barren and untended. Maybe, she thought now, the curse wasn't after John — maybe the curse *was* John, or something about him, carried by him, light as the scent of his Guerlain cologne.

When the other girls on the floor noticed her illness, her hand, they imagined food poisoning, the flu. "Let's get you to the nurse," they said, cooing in soft tones as they swaddled Mary in blankets and walked her to the campus clinic. But once there, Mary couldn't say what the matter was. She couldn't say anything at all.

The nurse prescribed aspirin and talk therapy, and Mary took both, finding herself a week later seated opposite Dr. Harris, a broad, brown-suited man with lines etched into his forehead like stacked horizons. He said very little during the hour, and so did she.

"Your silence suggests a manipulative character," he said, and after several sessions, Mary believed him. Whereas at first her voice had stuck in her throat like a sob each time she tried to speak, now she simply found she had nothing to say. Although her hand had thawed, her voice had frozen over. She was leaden.

Summer 1964. Mary stayed in New York for therapy, she said, but really it was for distance from John. He had stopped calling, and she was humiliated, revealed as a *slut* and, worse than that, a disposable one. And yet she missed him. His disappearance had peeled something, the scab over her mother wound, perhaps. It glowed now, undressed and septic. Maybe that's why, as time passed, Mary allowed the details of that night at the Plaza to soften in her memory. She obsessed over everything she'd said or done but brushed off John's brusqueness, the hot light of the room and the careless way he'd sent her off. She allowed herself to forget that afterward she'd suspected that *he* was the cursed one. She forgot, and so she wondered if his silence had something to do with her, how he'd plumbed her and found the rotten truth of who she was: the girl who'd run from her dying mother, who'd hidden behind the toolshed when Midge had whispered *Hide me,* the kind of girl who couldn't cry at her funeral.

She sublet a place on the Upper West Side from her old tutor, Mr. Smith. It was a dark, railroad-style one-bedroom stocked with books and little else. Tiny lamps lit her way around the place at night, but barely.

Evenings she walked down Broadway, heading to dates with friends of her friends' older brothers, boys she slept with and ran away from in the night. They rarely called afterward, although she wanted them to, searching as she was for someone to contradict the certainty of her badness.

More and more, Midge appeared in Mary's dreams as misplaced, tucked into the linen closet and forgotten, jumping forward in attack when Mary discovered her; or buried alive, her white fingers reaching up through the soil. Before bed every night, Mary swallowed double doses of aspirin to sleep deeper, to erase all thought and history.

Mornings she woke, then hid under the covers, her bed a raft she rode over oceans of unstructured time. Sometimes she stayed there all day, frozen. Sometimes she rose, forced to her feet by a restlessness she could exhaust only by walking. Up and down Manhattan in the short nightgown she wore as a dress — cream colored, with a Peter Pan collar and a pattern of red roses. She had straightened her hair on a whim that spring, waiting under the hairdryer at Lord & Taylor for hours while the chemicals set in and burned out the curls. Afterward she'd felt new, cleansed, her silky hair like poured thought, simple and pure. But the feeling had soon worn off, though she chased it, spending money on drinks and meals, meeting men. Maybe in them, she thought, she might find a way around John. Maybe they

131

wouldn't see in her what he had: something spoiled and easily controlled.

So she fucked the men, the boys, fucked them all. She fucked them in hotel rooms and in their clean apartments on the Upper East Side. She walked home to Mr. Smith's in the morning light, holding the hem of her baby-doll dress like an indecisive Kewpie, the sounds of the city waking up around her, all air brake and release, all garden hose watering the bodega blooms she passed as she walked up Broadway. Each time she returned to the apartment: the stale smell of old books and unemptied trash, as if she were returning to her own inner world. She accepted the decay but bathed and brushed her teeth compulsively. She heated the iron to flatten her hair. She examined her face in the mirror, sallow where once it had been flushed.

It began as a pimple, blossoming from the edge of her lower lip. Accompanied by a small lump beneath her chin, it grew. She charted its progress in the bathroom mirror, leaving, calling it nothing, then returning again to look, to feel, to imagine the cancer growing steadily, to imagine it expanding.

It had been days since she'd left the apartment. How could she? Look at this thing. The last time she went out, to visit a group of Sarah Lawrence girls living at the Barbizon Hotel, they'd patted zit cream and concealer on it, only a shadow then. *You poor thing,* they'd cooed, and she'd wanted to curl up and stay there, sublet be damned. *These* girls had done it right, with a series of connected rooms for the summer and internships in midtown. In the evenings they lay poolside, novels resting unread on their laps as they chatted. They ordered room service and ate spread-eagled on their fancy beds, complaining about their skin tones and tummy fat one minute, then slyly proposing late-night sundaes from the diner around the corner the next. But she'd made her bed, and now she must lie in it, she figured. So she returned home to Mr. Smith's apartment and heated up a can of Dinty Moore stew on the single-burner stove, lounging on the ratty sofa while she ate, a book propped open in front of her. It was silent in the apartment, and when she turned the pages, their thin flutter resounded.

The next day the pimple began to throb. When she examined it in the mirror, she felt the lump hardening. Immediately she thought of Midge: the mussel shell of malignancy in her left breast, the way it grew roots and spread throughout her body.

In the emergency room, an intern ran his cold and slender fingers over the thin skin of her throat. He shook his head and left, returning an hour later with his supervising physician. "Impetigo," the doctor said, exasperated, as if both Mary and the intern were overreacting. "That lump you feel is just a swollen gland." That was it. They gave her some salve and sent her home.

After that she stayed inside, mortified, watching the sore develop like some horrific creeping thing. It filled with purple blood and pus, engorging daily. She ate her stew, read her books. The city steamed and sang outside her windows.

It was late at night when the sore finally erupted, bursting like an artery, leaving behind a fleshy crater. Mary felt blood and pus trickling down the side of her face. A horror show. "I need you to come and get me," she pleaded to her father on the phone. "I need to leave this place. I need to leave this place now." She clutched the clunky black receiver like an anchor, hoping the weight of it might tether her. "What's wrong?" Bob asked her through the bewildered congestion of sleep. "I don't know I don't know I don't know," she repeated.

12

In the early 1960s, Jell-O's age-old selling point as a national beacon of stability, a staple of nuclear-family dinner tables and affordable "fancy" dishes, flickered and surged dramatically. This wasn't success: this was the gasp of a flame preparing to die out. The country was in flux, teetering on the latter half of a century that had inflicted trauma on the collective psyche. And now, America was in the middle of another war, facing stirrings of civil disobedience. Change was filtering into the country's unconscious, hinting of the upheaval soon to roil up, a fever from beneath our national skin. Advertisements responded as best they could. Best to hunker down for now, they urged, their messages achingly upbeat, like forced smiles: best to lean on routine and familiar family structures. Best to serve a delightful and wholesome Jell-O mold tonight. In new mixed-fruit, blackberry, and orange-banana flavors!

More than ever, family was a focal point. The family unit was to be stressed, preserved. So even as Jell-O advertisements kept a toe in the water of the diet conscious, they also revolved around the nightly dinner table, reflecting the indulgent side of America's cultural ethos. *There are people who like to eat,* one television spot began, speaking over a montage of different American dinner tables where a clan of Maine lobstermen shells the fruits of their labor, an Italian matriarch serves pasta, and a third family celebrates the oldest son's return from military service by heaping his plate with food. *There's Always Room for Jell-O!* the ad proclaims, even for those stuffed full of America's bounty.

America's tenuous bounty. By 1964 the beacon had gone out for LeRoy. In a move that would change the town forever, General Foods closed the original Jell-O factory and relocated manufacturing from New York to Delaware. Families who'd worked for Jell-O for generations were suddenly faced with an impossible choice: leave the only home they'd ever known, or lose their only job. Many LeRoy natives, so betrayed by Jell-O's departure, vowed never to buy it again. They knew what they'd had was special.

LeRoy's sudden crisis reflected a larger, national one: looming cultural and economic upheaval, an identity in limbo. Like many small towns in America, LeRoy was actively losing the jobs that had made it prosperous. They knew no magical mass-produced cash cow would come their way again. And although Haloid Xerox, Lapp Insulator, and Eastman Kodak, staples of Rochester's economy, mercifully stayed put (for the time being, however: Kodak laid off thousands of employees in 1997 and declared bankruptcy in 2012), the decampment of Jell-O marked the beginning of the end of the region's boom time.

The decline has been significant since then but drastic in the last decade. As recently as the 1980s, the median income in LeRoy was nearly 9 percent higher than the national average. Since then it has fallen to well below the national average. The stress of unemployment, specifically the loss of the factory work that once helped it prosper, performs itself in LeRoy through the transformation of the town's once-formidable homes — Gothic and Greek revival houses with butler's pantries and enough bedrooms for large families — into multi-unit rental properties. Families, too, have changed, their structure altering alongside the disappearance of factory work. In 1980, LeRoy had fewer single mothers than the rest of the country. But in the past thirty years, that number has surpassed the national average.

The absence of strong father figures and nuclear families in LeRoy would become, in 2011 and 2012, a talking point for journalists and doctors investigating the origins of the LeRoy girls' sickness. Financial instability and tenuous support systems were eventually targeted as key contributors to the girls' condition, which was, doctors argued, fundamentally rooted in deep insecurity and stress. But stress and insecurity were quickly ignored in favor of older, more familiar narratives concerning the dangers of female desire. Watered-down versions even appeared in popular novels such as Katherine Howe's *Conversion* and Megan Abbott's *The Fever,* both fictionalized accounts of the girls' illness. Where Howe's novel posits that the tics and twitches come from the history of the town (moved, in the novel, to Danvers, Massachusetts) as a site of witch trials, Abbott's *The Fever* frames the outbreak as a repercussion of the afflicted girls' burgeoning sexuality and the "increased physical vulnerability" that accompanies their transition from children into adolescents. Abbott suggests this change is "a kind of witchcraft," but by the end of the novel, the characters' symptoms are revealed to have been caused less by magic than by a mélange of poison — administered by one particularly jealous girl — deception, and mass psychogenic illness, which Abbott barely defines. The whole fever, it turns out, revolved primarily around competition for the attention of a popular boy.

This, of course, is a common story, that of malingering and manipulative women, their competition and precarious sexuality, which must be tamped down, contained, lest it lead to sickness, crime, catastrophe. This is also the story that the mothers of the real LeRoy girls rejected. Their daughters weren't faking, or poisoning each other; they weren't insanely jealous or sexually deviant. Nor were they victims of unstable home lives. Many of the mothers found themselves in the position of wearily defending their ability to single-parent — or to parent despite their own illness — asserting with understandable defensiveness that they, and they alone, could handle motherhood, breadwinning, and the onset of this outbreak. They'd always had to, after all,

and their daughters were stronger for it —
not weaker. So there must be a physical
origin to the girls' condition. Emotional
trauma couldn't touch these girls, their
mothers argued, because these girls had
been raised by women strong enough to
bear it.

Emotion as weakness, desire as instability,
trauma as failure: these correlations came
up often in regard to the girls of LeRoy.
These girls were strong, mothers insisted,
not traumatized. But the two are not mutu-
ally exclusive, my mother argued, even as
she wistfully doubted all the girls would get
the help they needed. "They need to express
themselves," she said, "but they don't live
in a culture that teaches them to." Trauma
needs to be spoken, she said, it needs to be
heard. The girls' conversion disorder was
essentially a coping mechanism, a system
their minds found to tolerate the intolerable
until they were able to find help. Disorder
is, she said, in its own way, an ingenuity.

13

ADMISSION REPORT: SEPTEMBER 2, 1964

This is the first psychiatric hospitalization for Mary Fussell, a nineteen-year-old, single college student who is referred to Austen Riggs by Dr. Berger of Rochester, New York, because of probable impending psychotic decompensation and a need for treatment away from her family. The patient's extended family background is a chaotic conglomeration of great wealth, marital strife, divorce, heavy drinking, suicide, and general unhappiness. As a child she was left to the care of a maid. Childhood difficulties included excessive dreaming, fear of the dark, and fear of school.

The patient dates the onset of her current problems to age fourteen, when she started prep school at Kent Place School in Summit, New Jersey. This was several months after her mother died of cancer of the breast. At this time she began to feel that everything and everybody was unreal and she did not belong anywhere. She became increasingly tense, had severe spells of depression and difficulty controlling her temper. She was a leader of rebels against school traditions. As these symptoms worsened she began to drink sporadically but heavily for relief. She became increasingly tense, fearful, insomniac, suffered terrifying hypnogogic states, and had episodes when she felt as if she were "falling apart."

Mary made herself small on the bed, knees

bent and pulled in, arms wrapped around her shins. She was in her nightgown now, the baggy clothes she'd worn all day in a careless pile on the floor. She hadn't bathed yet. She could smell herself, contaminated by her own sweat and juices, and for once it didn't matter. It was over, all that effort. She was here, she had arrived, and she didn't have to do anything.

Here was the Austen Riggs Center, the open psychiatric center in Stockbridge, Massachusetts, where she'd wound up after Bob fetched her from Manhattan and installed her back in LeRoy. She'd only worsened there, confined to the East Main Street house, holed up in her room, hiding from Cousin John, who had assumed his usual cheerful persona, sitting in his favorite chair in the living room as if nothing had happened. He'd even placed his hand on her knee once when they were alone. But at his touch, Mary felt her body begin to freeze. It was suddenly as if the whole of her had been sat on, trapped beneath a heavy weight, each limb numb and bloodless. She wanted to say something but couldn't find her voice. It was stuck beneath her solar plexus, squeezing. This was a feeling she was getting used to: the sensation of drowning any time she tried to speak, her lungs flooding with imagined fluid. When her father walked in, it took everything she had to force herself to stand and leave the room. Finally Bob drove Mary to a shrink in Rochester, who frowned as he checked her arms for track marks, then picked up his phone, covering the receiver to tell her he was calling the Austen Riggs Center — she needed immediate hospitalization.

That morning, Mary's first at Riggs, she'd met with the therapist assigned to her, Dr. Marcus, who sat in his wing-backed chair with his legs crossed, a clipboard in his lap, waiting for her to speak. But she'd been unable to begin, unsure of what to say about her life since her mother's death. Everything since she'd hidden from Midge's pleas had been ugly and shameful. She didn't want to expose herself this way to Dr. Marcus, who was young and handsome, like John. She wanted him to think her beautiful, as John had. She wanted him to prove something, something salvageable, redeemable, about her, despite her problems.

After her silent session, Mary had walked into town for cigarettes. Now she was alone in her blue-walled room, sitting on her bed, chain-smoking and thinking about dinner. But to eat alone, all those eyes on her — the new girl? She pulled a Parliament from the carton, stared at the bunch of sheets around her ankles as she smoked, looking up when the roll of a clear glass bottle clinked against the wood of her bedroom door.

It was almost empty. A moment later, her door was pushed open. "Yoo-hoo," someone said. The voice was female and gravelly. Mary cleared her throat, and in came a short girl in a marigold turban and a gray poncho, her right hand wrapped around the neck of another bottle. "Care for a drink?" she said, grinning and bad.

Bea's body filled every room she entered. The smell of patchouli and vodka preceded her coming, Joplinesque, through every doorway, staggering with grace over every threshold. The night they met, she sat on the edge of Mary's bed with her legs splayed wide and a bottle propped against her crotch. She poured two paper cups to the halfway mark while Mary waved her hand, a gesture of refusal. "I'm trying not to drink," she said.

Bea's eyes widened. "Whatever for?" she asked, her voice breathy.

"I think it's making me sicker," Mary said.

"That's ridiculous," Bea said. "Don't be a wimp." She held out a cup, giving it a little waggle for every second Mary hesitated.

When Mary took the cup, Bea sat back, satisfied, and sipped hers in between drags of a long white cigarette. She smoked Kools, and they suited her. Mary felt timid in her presence and held her cup with both palms wrapped around its cylindrical body.

"I thought drinking was against the rules," she said. Bea shrugged.

"Everyone does it."

The warm liquid burned Mary's throat when she swallowed, a familiar sort of singeing. A cleansing. She was disappointed. She'd thought the rules would be firmer here, the boundaries surer.

"So, what's your deal?" Bea asked, taking a sip.

"I don't know," Mary said. "Well, Jell-O." She started there.

"No fucking way," Bea said, lifting her eyebrows, as if it meant everything. "Jell-O?" The product was fast-tracked to become the epitome of uncool, a symbol of the suburban establishment. She put her cup between her thighs and fiddled with her turban. "You *square,*" she said. Mary looked at her cup, ashamed. But Bea shook her head and said *Wow, honey* when she heard about Midge's death, about Cousin John, about the Dex coursing, even now, through

Mary's veins. Bea wasn't impressed by the drugs; she approved of them. Most of all, she approved of *Mary*. When Mary said she wanted to quit them, too, Bea shook her head. "Don't," she said. "Everybody needs somewhere they can escape to."

In the end, they talked all night. They went over Mary's family, Bea's. They talked about Riggs and its rules — or lack thereof. They ran over the list of its oddball patients, which included, ironically, Norman Rockwell. He lived in Stockbridge.

"I see him sometimes," Bea said, "moping around town."

"Not as cheerful as his paintings," she said when Mary looked shocked. "But then," she added, "who is?"

The girls met in the hallway the next morning, hungover and tired. "Take a nap later," Bea commanded. "Tonight we go to Simm's."

Mary had known Bea less than twenty-four hours, but she could already see that Simm's was an obsession of hers. Simm's this, Simm's that. "Everybody goes to Simm's," Bea said through the cigarette stuck in between her lips, coiling the fringed shawl around her neck as she led Mary through the autumn night. "That's where the boys hang out."

The boys were Hollis and Tim, opposite but for the matching biker jackets they wore, their bodies soft like slugs beneath their leather shells. Hollis was aloof, apathetic. He turned up the collar of his jacket, rolled the sleeves over twice. Tim was shy, insecure. "He's the sensitive type," Bea said, kissing his cheek. "I think you two will get along." They did, two nights later, a gentle fuck, hesitant, then desperate. After that Tim tucked Mary beneath his leather wing like she was something to be careful with.

She was fragile. But her admission to Riggs had been on a trial basis. All patients began this way, tentatively. Mary knew she was sick. But how sick? Sick enough to stay at Riggs, she hoped, where she finally felt safe.

It wasn't just safety Riggs offered. It was a sense of being believed. Her disorder, the disorder of her, made some kind of order there. The men she'd dated in New York. Cousin John. Tom. Even her father. None of them saw she was struggling. None of them seemed to care. "Take a trip to Europe," Bob had advised the night before she left for Riggs. "You need perspective, not the loony bin." But Mary had insisted, looking at her knees and shaking her head. She

148

knew perspective would come from structure and also from someone to talk to.

She waited out the diagnostic period nervously, holding the hem of her beloved baby-doll dress, fraying its edges. She pulled her hair obsessively, starting at the root and working down the strands like she was trying to coax everything straight. "Stop worrying about it," Bea kept telling her as the trial time ran out. "You're sick enough, okay?" Mary stared at her with an expression both confused and meek, and Bea smoothed her hair like a mother. "There, there," she'd say. "I don't waste my time on the healthy ones."

The day of Mary's admission conference, they sat together outside Dr. Marcus's office. Bea had her arm hooked around Mary's elbow, steadying her as she rocked in her seat, chanting nursery rhymes and looking at the ceiling. Bea pinched her arm.

"Come off it, Fussell," she said. "You're crazy, but not completely nuts. . . . Here." She placed a cigarette gently in between Mary's lips and struck a match.

On the other side of the wall, Mary could almost hear the men talking about her, saying her name. "They order lunch," Bea snorted, "and make a real day of it." Mary imagined the doctors in there, chewing. She pictured Dr. Marcus wiping his mouth with a corner of his napkin before placing it back in his lap.

"You know, a few months ago some guy sent a cake to his conference," Bea said. "On it he'd written in pink icing, *Please Be Kind.*"

"Did it work?"

"Hell no. They sent that crazy to McLean."

"Maybe I should have tried an offering of Jell-O," Mary quipped. "A big pink mold of my brain for them to eat." They laughed just as the door opened.

"Mary?" Dr. Marcus said. "You can come in now."

ADMISSION CONFERENCE: OCTOBER
    5, 1964

Mary is a tall, slim, attractive young lady who comes to
appointments dressed in ragged
denim Bermuda shorts and an
oversized rumpled cardigan.
She sits rigidly huddled in
her chair with her legs
tightly crossed and arms

150

folded over her chest, as if holding herself in check at the same time she shuts out the world. She is capable of abrupt, dramatic changes in appearance and affect, which appear unrelated to any external stimulus. Usually, she looks sad, puzzled and apathetic. Intermittently, she ceases all movement and, virtually frozen, stares as if terrified; then her whole body jerks violently and she resumes her previous posture.

DEVELOPMENTAL HISTORY:

As a little girl Mary was bold, active, and aggressive. She was more adventurous and quick to learn than her brother, who was privileged to receive more care and attention than she. Neither parent spent much time with the children. Her father was on three- to four-day flying assignments. During periods of free time he and his wife went to wild parties, usually leaving home in the late afternoon, returning about four in the morning and sleeping until noon. There was nobody to make sense of the world. A house came to represent Mary's only stable, reliable object.

Mary often played alone but preferred to play with her brother and his pals, who treated her like a scapegoat until age ten, when they developed a sexual interest in her. Often these boys would come into her bedroom, wake her up, and fondle and experiment with her. During this time Mary's most frequent and pleasant daydream was of building a large house.

On April 9, 1959 (age fourteen), Mary's mother died. After her mother's death Mary reports to have cried just once.

PSYCHOLOGICAL TEST REPORT:
This is an unusually angry young woman. She assumes a disdainful, cynical stance,

giving vent to her inner sense of bitterness and pessimism. Coupled with this is her sense of futility about anything being worthwhile. Feelings of helplessness, despair, and isolation are prominent. At the same time she defensively maintains a hard, shell-like exterior, refusing to allow herself to be caught up in sentimentality.

Overall, the patient has a negative view of herself as an ugly, unappealing person, and, consistent with this, there are strong needs to reject femininity in herself, for her concept of feminine sexuality is surrounded by sadomasochistic notions. She sees women as damaged and injured, malevolent and ungiving, and men as unresponsive and devilishly evil.

DIAGNOSIS:
Borderline schizophrenia with marked depressive and hysterical features in a

schizoid, narcissistic character.

From her spot on the sofa, Mary could see
out the window and across the lawn. The
clock ticked, counting out the hour. Smoke
from her cigarette entwined with Dr. Marcus's. "Mary," he said. She was on her back
in the grass, sinking corpselike into the
earth, where she'd be mothered and held.
She was sinking, sinking. She could hear his
voice, but dimly, *Mary, Mary,* calling her
back to the room, to her body, which froze
and seized at times like this, a process she
felt but couldn't stop. The seizures were as
unpredictable and erratic as her mood,
which wavered from day to day, not in little
ticks but in grand swings, an atmospheric
pressure needle seesawing uncontrollably
on a plummeting airplane.

The drinking didn't help. It started every
day at four, with Bea's arrival at her room.
Before dinner they'd sit by Mary's mirror
and examine their faces. They didn't wear
makeup. It wasn't their thing, hippies that
they were. But Bea played with Mary's hair,
arranging it in a loose pile atop her head
before letting it fall around her face. She
pinched her cheeks and lips to pull the red
out. Mary was Bea's porcelain doll, holding

out her glass palms for the pills Bea tipped into them, parting her lips for the color Bea painted.

Once primped, the girls walked to Simm's arm in arm, sister witches singing Jefferson Airplane up at the stars, the dark sky strobing crystalline points down on their zigzag path. Their voices cut the cold with puffs of hot breath. Mary wore her baby-doll dress and a long ratty sweater, even in the dead of winter. Bea wore the white feather boa she liked wrapped tight around her neck. It always wound up slipping, wagging like a tail behind her.

Together, Mary and Bea were witches. But their magic was vague, as was their desire. All Mary knew was that she wanted to be wanted. The rest she could take or leave. Bea seemed less interested in being chosen. "We're not possessive here," she often said, swaying in her chair. But Mary *wanted* to be possessed. She wanted containment and safety. Sex was just a numbness she rode out from a detached perch somewhere on the ceiling, somewhere outside her body. Even with Tim, who was gentle and concerned, she felt disassociated. It was the affection, the afterglow, she craved.

Mary pined for stability. She wanted to go back and do her childhood over again, get it right this time. If only she'd known not to pester Tom so. If only she'd fended off his friends. If only she'd been the perfect daughter, compliant and quiet and brave. Maybe then Midge would still be alive. Or Elfrida. Maybe then Cousin Joan wouldn't have disappeared. Maybe then there'd be someone to nurture her. But all she had was Bea, who was a fickle mother, jealous and harsh at times, absent others. Of course there was love, too. There were the times Bea tucked Mary into bed, then sat on the edge, promising to stay through the night. "I'll never leave you, Fussell," she swore, whispering *I'm right here, I'm right here,* as she smoothed Mary's hair, a mantra cast out into anxious waters, that Mary clung to like a buoy. On nights like these, Bea saved her. But it never lasted long. Bea always let her down eventually, disappearing into Hollis's room and the heroin he kept there, leaving Mary alone for long hours with only her bourbon and Dex to cleave herself from her mother's ghost.

Fridays after community meetings, Bea and Mary, Hollis and Tim, met in the parking lot to make a weekend plan. Where to go, what to do? Get high and walk around the botanical gardens? Drive to Boston, Northampton, or New York? The cities often won out, and the group would pile into Hollis's Corvair, dropping Dex before they hit the highway, then watching out the windows as the world flew by, a blur of feathery green.

One autumn night, they got high at the entrance of the Taconic and then made for New York. Mary sat in the backseat, talking frantically, caressing strips of her hair. Bea put her hand on Mary's forehead, pulled her torso into the scoop of her armpit and breast, and she quieted like a child, watching out the window as the landscape peeled past them and around them. Hollis pushed the Corvair past sixty, moving them through space with the effortlessness of drugs hitting blood, of skylines opening, a shock of skyscrapers, cold and gray after so much green.

"So," Bea said as they merged into city traffic, snaking along the west side, small and white in the shadows of gray. "You guys ready for some real action?"

Nobody replied. The car was silent, each passenger a singular, brewing storm. Mary felt prudish and small. She didn't want to say it, but she was scared.

They parked around the corner from the Bitter End. Hollis pulled something small from under the seat. "Let's go," he said. Bea and Mary linked arms automatically and followed the boys along Bleecker and up MacDougal, where Hollis stopped at a dingy walk-up. "Be cool," he said, looking at Tim, who then looked at the girls. Bea unlaced her arm from Mary's and walked confidently around Tim to follow Hollis. Mary paused at the foot of the stairs, which were too narrow to climb in twos. She thought about turning around and walking out the door. She *could* be in the city by herself, after all. Since admitting herself to Riggs, since attaching to Bea, she'd almost forgotten her own self-sufficiency. She often felt like she needed Bea's input for even the simplest things: when to eat dinner, when to go to bed, and what to do when she awoke. She feared displeasing her almost as much as she feared the memory of her mother's abandonment, her sudden disappearance into death.

"Fussell!" Bea yelled from the top of the stairs, shattering Mary's indecision. "Stop fucking around." Her tone was cutting, as if she were berating a lazy child. Bea, easygoing on the outside, was controlling and high strung within. Mary saw now how everything about Bea confirmed Mary's sense of smallness and silence, how their friendship had silenced her. She'd come to

Riggs wanting order and rules, and she'd found them, but not in the right place. Bea wasn't a therapist. She was an addict, and her future was exactly what Mary was trying to escape. Mary climbed the stairs, ears ringing with the truth of her realization, vision blurred and stinging in the dim tobacco light.

On the third floor, Hollis stood outside an orange door. When Mary joined the group assembled on the landing, he knocked three times. The dented metal door swung open, pulled by an invisible hand.

Inside, the walls were stark and white, with yellow stains along the baseboard. There was a twin mattress on the floor. Three girls were flopped, half-naked on its bare white and blue. A sheet was balled up and tossed into a corner. A tray of needles balanced precariously on the armrest of a stained sofa.

The room seemed to tick with the pulse of so many fluid-filled veins, each heartbeat a second count, measuring the silence. Hollis counted bills, and the *flip-flip* of the crisp paper made the place smell fresh and green. On the mattress by Mary's feet, a girl hummed Jefferson Airplane through her blue corpse lips. The light filtered through the colored scarves tacked up over the windows. The heat pipes clanged deep inside the walls. The needles were offered, served up like hors d'oeuvres.

When Bea poked the needle into Mary's arm, the skin resisted, as if in protest, before giving way to droplets of red, a blue bruise blooming almost instantly from the site of insertion. Bea began to lightly push the trigger. "Breathe, Fussell," she said without kindness. Mary looked away, at the sprawled-out girls, dead-eyed and painless. She felt a chill enter her bloodstream, washing into her body. She thought of it, this poison she was allowing inside her. Everything she'd done with Bea since arriving at Riggs had been this way, venom sweetened by belonging. *Poison poison poison* pulsed in her head. She felt her chest begin to shrink, her arm begin to freeze into the witch's hand, gnarled and rotten. *No!* she thought, her body suddenly twitching, bucking involuntarily, an unissued scream. Her arm swung forward, knocking into Bea's shoulder and breast and throwing the needle across the room. "Fucking Christ," Bea yelled as the boys scampered to retrieve the syringe.

The group's ejection from the apartment

was swift after that. Outbursts from new girls weren't allowed; the deal was off. Nobody wanted yells traced back to the den, nobody wanted to call attention to its moist-aired cocoon. Mary begged for forgiveness, but the damage was done. Bea was withdrawing — she could feel that female solidarity shrinking — and Mary sensed something immutable had passed between them. The price of Bea's friendship had always been adherence to her rules, rules Mary had now violated.

Monday after the drug run. Mary climbed the stairs to Dr. Marcus, pulling back on the banister with each step, as if she might fall if she simply let go. "You're awfully quiet today, Mary," Dr. Marcus said after half the session passed in silence. "May I ask how your weekend was?"

"I don't know."

She kept her eyes on the rug at her feet, green and gold and so clean-edged where it met the dark wood floor it covered. She considered saying something about the heaviness she'd woken up with, a sense of numbed-out loss. Everything would be different now. Even if Mary wanted to return to Bea's good graces, she couldn't. She knew now she needed safety and structure.

The rules at Riggs were a spell she'd have to follow in order to discover what the curse really was and, in the process, to break it. But Bea wouldn't understand; she had settled here, a permanent guest. Mary still wanted a life in the outside world. She was willing to do whatever she had to in order to get it.

She thought all this but couldn't say it. Instead she receded into her body, frozen and unfeeling. She could hear Dr. Marcus saying *Mary Mary Mary,* but her voice was locked inside her. In the circles and pock-marks of the wooden door, she saw her mother's face, the shape of her dying body dissolving in downward lines like the corpses of Palermo, shelved into stone walls like books. Only one thing filtered in, only one thing got through: death and its inevita-bility, the indelible badness she'd imprinted upon herself the day Midge left for the hospital, left for her death; the day Mary had been too cowardly to help her hide from it. So how could she tell Dr. Marcus what had happened in New York? How could she betray her friend, turning her in to the authorities at Riggs the way she turned her mother in to the paramedics? *Be absolutely silent,* Midge's image told her now. *If you talk, someone dies.*

Someone dies, gets sick, and jumps. In a white nightgown, her body a dove, open winged and free. "Your cousin Joan," Dr. Marcus was saying, "your father thought you should know." He touched her arm. "Mary, nod if you understand me." She tried to look at him and signal that she understood. But she couldn't. Her body was immobile, her mind building the scene: Joan in her bedclothes, just discharged from a mental hospital with only a private nurse to watch over her. The nurse on a cigarette break, or in the bathroom. The open window, the flight.

"Mary," Marcus said again, but she was picturing the tip of Joan's cigarette, the angel-heart ember, the way it had ebbed and flowed like a beacon with the warmth of Joan's breath. She was making a list in her mind, cataloging the other people who'd died, tallying names like they'd add up to an answer. Aunt Edith and Elfrida, Midge and Joan. The sum of their absence was the sum of everything she feared. Each loss, each death, showed her own death, its inescapability, its predatory nature, how it was coming for her, cutting through everyone she loved on its way with its mean, exacting disorder. "Mary," Dr. Marcus said over and over again, calling her back. Her name was an incantation. But now she was shaking, arms frozen by her side, gaze fixed like she was looking beyond the room at something immaterial, death itself, perhaps, or time, the ticking seconds designed to measure out a life she knew was already lost.

She didn't attend the funeral a week later. She didn't want to see John, or return to LeRoy, where everything felt predicated on her silence. Once she had believed the curse was strongest there. Now she was more confused than ever about what the curse truly was. She was sure now that Cousin John had been wrong; it was the women, not the men, who suffered. But why? What was it that afflicted them so? Something to do with LeRoy, the dullness and rules she'd sensed even as a child? Or something wider, more insidious? She thought of Midge, Elfrida, and Joan, searching her memory for clues. She thought of her summer in Manhattan, how even there she'd felt something stifling her. Even *now,* after the drug run, after Bea's distance, Mary felt as if she were fighting for her life. No, better not return. Better to stay in bed, covered up and hidden.

When Bea came to visit, Mary accepted her

awkward coos, but with a new sense of reserve. She wouldn't speak, just shook her head yes and no. And when Bea asked her careful questions — "Do you need anything?" — Mary couldn't help but think there was nothing Bea could give. Her answer had always been reliably simple: another drink, a needle, a pill.

"Okay then, Fussell," Bea said, a hint of exasperation in her voice as she left Mary's room. "I'm going to New York with Hollis," she said on her way out. She lingered in the doorway, hesitating for a moment before walking through the door. "Be back in a few days," she said over her shoulder.

Maybe she'd been too harsh, freezing her out. But as time passed after the botched drug run and Bea's departure, Mary slept better. She got better at waking herself from nightmares. She read. She drank red wine from a tannin-tinged cup she'd long ago filched from the dining hall. She walked in the fall drizzle, gazing at the gray sky, the red leaves so brilliant they seemed accidental, like beautiful stains. She thought about Bea. She wondered if she could save their friendship after all.

One night the rain picked up, and she ducked into Simm's, cold and wet. She straddled a barstool, picked peanuts from a metal bowl, and ordered a bourbon. She sipped, the liquor warm and soothing as it made its way inside her.

"Mary," someone said, and she swung around in her seat, startled by the crowd suddenly gathered around her. Everyone was speaking at once, voices panicked and rushed. She was hazy, her brain slow. *What are they saying?* Something about rain on the Taconic, the tinny body of a car wrapped around a tree trunk. Something about the body of a girl trapped between metal and wood. Mary held out her hands, opening her palms and pushing at the air, her gesture like brakes pumping. *Slow down. What?* "Bea's dead," somebody said.

In an instant Mary knew it was true, knew it because of the blood behind her eyelids, shading everything a blotchy red, like the circles of stick and essence stained on Bea's fur coat, rain soaked when they pulled her from the wreck. She had lived a while afterward, someone added. The cops had said she was a nice girl.

14

In the late 1960s, as Mary entered her mid-twenties, as she mourned her best friend, Bea, her cousin Joan, and her mother, Midge, the country transformed. The divorce rate crept up, preparing to skyrocket in the mid-seventies. The Vietnam War raged. Women raised on the rhetoric of the domestic-science movement left the home to protest and to work. Proper housekeeping and the preservation of the nuclear family were no longer paramount; the 1950s were *over,* and with them went all the effort Americans had poured into managing and forgetting wartime trauma. Early in the decade, Jell-O had urged normalcy and routine, leaning on the importance of domesticity to assure Americans that a well-kept home in a well-kept country would keep trauma a distant, ever-fading memory. But now America was knee-deep in another war, packing up children and sending them off to risk death. How could anything be routine at a time like this? Domestic science had been roundly wrong, Americans realized. The doctrine of technologically advanced housework was simply an instrument in capitalism's grand scheme to sell neatly packaged imitation products promising the American Dream. Perhaps the dream itself was the problem.

Women's particular dissatisfaction with their old roles proved a serious adjustment for companies like Jell-O, who were accustomed to profiting off women's imperative to be the perfect housekeeper and wife. How to reach an audience newly interested in natural foods? What about those concerned that Jell-O was the domain of old folks and squares? What about the growing population of divorcées, back to work and back to dating? Maybe, ads suggested, women such as this could just sprinkle Jell-O powder on yogurt, cupcakes, ice cream, and fruit? Would that be too much to ask? Or perhaps they would consider returning to the kitchen if reminded of how happy it made everyone else. *Make Someone Happy,* advertisements urged, reminding women of their roles. *Make Someone Jell-O.*

It seemed, however, that these admonishments fell on deaf ears. So Jell-O tried again. *Somehow It's Always Right,* a 1971 slogan assured as the company struggled to keep up with the changing times. But marketing to women outside the scaffolding of domestic duty proved a challenge, and sales waned.

And then came an ill-fated series of print ads from the 1970s, pointed, I guess, at cheekiness. The ads feature close-ups of different women's faces as they hold different variations on Jell-O pudding up to the camera, angled above them. The adjacent text is in quotation marks, as if spoken to a husband. One woman looks guilty and holds her pink-nailed hand over her mouth like a naughty girl as she offers up a slice of Jell-O pecan pie, made with vanilla pudding. This, the advertisement states, is the *"Guess what happened when I backed the car out of the driveway, dear"* pudding. In another, identically formatted advertisement, a woman wears a fur coat, price tag prominently displayed, and presents the *"Notice anything different about me tonight, dear?"* pudding. Next we have the *"Congratulations, dear, but what exactly does a vice president do?"* pudding, offered by a young brunette, her eyebrows raised and her eyes opened wide, in a pantomime of dumb curiosity. The final ad in this unfortunate vein features a slightly older woman, one who has perhaps birthed and raised and released children into the world. She looks hopefully up at the camera as she holds out a slice of Jell-O chocolate cheesecake. This is the *"Dear, don't you think I'd be a more interesting person if I went to work?"* pudding.

Women didn't buy Jell-O's latest sales pitch, apparently. Sales remained in a slump. They knew they'd be more interesting outside the house and were done asking their husband for permission to leave.

So *The New Joys of Jell-O* — a revision to the popular 1961 cookbook — marketed itself to *independent* women, women advertisements portrayed out to lunch in urban landscapes, gelatin salad Niçoise and salmon mousse on their plates. For the hippie audience, a Green Goddess Salad Bowl also graced the pages, the recipe calling for a mixture of lime gelatin, garlic, sour cream, mayo, and anchovies, to be garnished with crabmeat. Although far from natural, the recipe gestures at a growing cultural interest in health food, particularly given its presentation, the pale-green Jell-O portion cut into thick cubes resembling avocado. Maybe, advertisements and recipes suggested, the Jell-O that had once so pointedly masked and molded natural ingredients could now celebrate them, connecting women to nature and to each other. The impulse, though understandable, was a failure. Jell-O, with its dyes and chemicals, could never make it as a natural food. The era of imitation foods had disappeared with the 1950s, and the dessert again found itself in need of a new angle, a new avenue by which to reach its target audience: women. But what did the newly liberated, newly single women of America want?

This was the research question posed by Betty Friedan, a wife, mother, and scholar who in 1952, during her second pregnancy, lost her job and devoted herself to stay-at-home motherhood. In her new role, Friedan found an emptiness she couldn't peg, a question she feared asking: *Is this all?*

Among Friedan's theories in *The Feminine Mystique* was the notion of a myth around womanhood, constructed and perpetuated by all-male advertising agencies and magazine editors. Every day, Friedan wrote, women sat down to watch TV, or read their newspapers and magazines, and were faced with the heavy-handed reminder that *all women* were either fulfilled as homemakers or miserable in their careers outside the home. There appeared to be no in-between.

But what if there could be? she asked, and her question became the fertile soil in which second-wave feminism took root. Not surprisingly, second wavers developed a vehement response to domestic science even as they ignored any headway the movement had made. In reducing the domestic-science movement to a pawn in patriarchy's game, feminists overlooked the radical yet rational approach it had taken, over decades, to empowering women. Empowering women in theory, anyway.

Early proponents of domestic science sought to alleviate food insecurity among America's impoverished population through mass-produced, nutritionally balanced food items, and to access modern science, technology, and creativity within the "feminine sphere," the only space, they believed, in which they'd have a fighting chance of doing so. And to a certain extent, women *did* gain power from the domestic-science movement. Kitchens and home economics classrooms were opened to them and became, for a short time, spaces in which they could experiment and create, if only in a culinary fashion. At its best, domestic science connected women to each other. So it was only natural for nostalgia to set in as Americans entered the 1970s and reflected on their newly shifted societal landscape. And it was onto this nostalgia that Jell-O attached, finally finding the marketing strategy that would carry it into the future.

"To give salads a holiday look," a disembodied male voice says in a Jell-O commercial from 1973, "start with Jell-O gelatin." As he speaks, viewers watch a busy brunette mom shepherd kids in the front door of a brownstone, drop her briefcase with a sigh, and remove her coat. This is *Mrs. Susan Dando of Boston,* we learn.

"This time of year we have friends over more than ever," Susan says, speaking to the camera, "and I like to do special things for them like my mother did for her friends." This, she continues, is easier than she'd previously thought. She quickly models the Jell-O mold recipe her mother made — cherry flavor impressed with nuts and slices of peach. Mrs. Dando surveys her work. An expression of wistful satisfaction passes over her face. "This looks beautiful," a guest remarks in the next scene as she accepts a plate and affirms the culinary capabilities of her friend. Mrs. Susan Dando of Boston is a busy working mother. But she still finds time to make the Jell-O she enjoyed as a girl, returning each year to the recipe that reconnects her to an absent mother. Perhaps it is a ritual for her, the ad suggests, especially when holiday grief overwhelms, to perform the caretaking activities her mother enjoyed, slipping into her mother's role, her mother's recipe, just as she might slip into a housecoat. Perhaps it is a comfort.

■ ■ ■ ■

BOOK II

■ ■ ■ ■

15

By 1982, Mary had found some semblance of order. After Bea's death, she'd followed the rules at Riggs, and though she'd never quite found her voice in therapy, nor figured out the meaning of the curse, after two years of treatment she was ready to reenter the world.

Before leaving Riggs, Mary had reconnected with boarding-school Judy. It was obvious to both women that they shared something, the knowledge of motherless girlhood, the knowledge of grief. They could never undo this bond, but they could depend on it. In reclaiming their friendship, they gave each other what a mother might: the courage to move fully into the lives they wanted. Judy urged Mary to finish her degree, and in 1969 she did, living in Vermont for a year while she studied studio art at Bennington, and then in Boston, where she received her MFA. After that was

New York, where she shared an apartment with Judy on the Upper West Side and built sets for off-Broadway shows. Judy had become a lead lighting designer, and the two wound up touring Europe with Emerson, Lake and Palmer, doing set design and lighting.

From time to time over the years Mary had returned to LeRoy to see Bob, who was remarried to the ex-wife of an old Panagra buddy. When Cousin John fell ill in the late seventies, she'd flown to Rochester to see him once more. "You were the one, Mona," he'd croaked from his sickbed, his eyes blurry with morphine and light. She'd felt shocked and thrilled. Once, John's approval had been the ultimate accomplishment, and for a brief moment she'd let herself beam with pride, as if she'd just won a precious award. But then she'd caught herself. What was she thinking? John's regard wasn't where her worth resided — all the psychoanalysis she'd done since leaving LeRoy should have at least taught her this. And how easily she was reeled back in. The thought of her own weakness made her nauseous, her insides acidic. She had to get out of there. "Rest now," she told John as she backed from his room.

Soon after John's death, Mary left the city for a cottage, following Judy to Short Beach, a boozy strip of land along Long Island Sound, just north of New Haven. She still drank to excess and slept around, but she also kept a studio in New Haven and went three times a week to therapy with a Jungian named Ray, who told her myths of mother goddesses and witches and suggested they work to heal the Bad Mother archetype within her. "Tell me everything," he said, and Mary, finally, spoke.

As her work with Ray progressed, Mary read all of Jung, then moved on to feminist revisions of the Bible. She read of witchcraft and goddess worship, she learned practical spell work to protect herself. She lay in bed in her cottage one night, glasses sliding down her nose, Adrienne Rich open on her lap, and read of a power that "permeates everything, even the language in which we try to describe it. It is diffuse and concrete; symbolic and literal; universal and expressed with local variations which obscure its universality." She sat up and bent over the book, rereading the lines. This was it, she realized in a dumbfounded flourish of relief;

how could she have missed it all this time? *This* was the curse, the very curse she'd built her life around avoiding. And it wasn't confined to her family. No, the curse was felt by others, *named* by others. The curse was patriarchy, and, as my mother would later write to me, the patriarchal temperature was high in her family, in Jell-O, and in LeRoy, birthplace of America's Most Famous Dessert, gravesite of the country's first women's university.

After that, Mary consumed every feminist text she could get her hands on. Evenings she sat out on her porch and read, caring for herself with books and stories and language, just as she had as a girl. But she needed something else, she decided, something other than herself to think of. So she bought Lilly, a standard poodle puppy with a mass of brown curls that matched her own, and treated her like a daughter, taking her for long walks on the salt marshes every day, then bathing her in the tub, cooing as she scrubbed.

Enter the man: my father. At the time, he lived next door with a golden retriever and a girlfriend named Peg. He was blond and tall and thin, with shoulder-length hair, aviator sunglasses he never took off, and a dented Porsche he drove too fast through the stoned beach community. It seemed he was always leaving, tearing off late for work in the mornings, or after an argument at night, the screen door slamming in his wake, its tinny closure reverberating. It wasn't her business, Mary told herself.

Sometimes she and Lilly would pass the man and his retriever on the beach, walking in the opposite direction, and the two dogs would sniff around each other, then leap into play. "I'd be happy to take her out with us during the day," Mary said, gesturing at the dog. "Anytime," she added for good measure, trying not to seem too eager. He thanked her, took off his glasses, and held out his hand. "George," he said.

They met again at a wedding after they'd each moved away. Mary wore a pink sun hat, a cream-colored dress she belted at the waist with an old scarf. The hat cast a wide-brimmed shadow over her face. Sunlight picked up hints of red in her hair. She smiled. She sipped. She was not yet drunk — she'd learned long ago how to pace herself — but she was relaxed. George wore a beige suit, tucked his shoulder-length hair behind his ears. He drank from a sweating bottle of beer, holding it lightly by the neck.

It had been a year since he last saw her, and now, in the quiet light of the summer evening, he was struck by her beauty all over again. She was stunning, small-waisted and soft-breasted, with long auburn curls haloing her face.

They talked about where they'd ended up, Mary a few towns over in an old farmhouse by the water with a chicken coop out back and a barn for her art; George in a bachelor pad. "I've always wanted to build a big house," she told him, "but I've settled for just rebuilding one."

When he saw the place for himself, later that night, he rocked his weight to his heels, placed his hands in his pockets. He looked almost hungrily through the dark at the peeling barn, the chipped drywall, the color-splashed canvases and red- and blue- and gold-stained glass, the sculpture. Mary's artwork had changed since she left Riggs. In place of the nightmares she'd shaped before, she was working now on a series of nurturing female shapes. Zaftig women giving birth, dancing en masse, a naked coven, howling beneath a low-slung moon. These were the women she'd admired as a child, the European mother-witches she'd always related to. These were the women she would work toward for the rest of her life.

■ ■ ■ ■

After that Mary and George were often together. They took dog walks every other day, made dinner in Mary's new kitchen. George moved in. He fixed things around the house. Mary cleared the table, rinsed wineglasses, turned them mouth down on dishrags to dry. They'd linger then, talking about their families: George's father, wealthy and excessive, who wrapped Jaguars around trees in blackout drunk after blackout drunk, who went to rehab multiple times before it stuck, before he became a spokesman for AA and helped others do the same; and Mary's: LeRoy and Cousin John; the Jell-O money she lived off of, the hold she felt it had on her, tethering her to her family even as it afforded her the freedom to paint.

This relationship, between Mary and money, dependence and freedom — would push and pull at her for the rest of her life. I saw its grip on her until the very end. She was incredibly fortunate; to that she would anxiously admit. She had a freedom most artists never have: the freedom to make her art outside the economic hardship of the artist's life. She could be a nonconformist and keep her house, her studio, her picket fence. She could afford to have me and pay for my day care so that she could work. But could she truly be a feminist? Could she truly resist the curse of patriarchy when she depended on a fortune built by patriarchal ideals? She felt guilty for this, as if she'd cheated. She'd never *had* to work. She'd never proven to herself that her work could make it. Maybe this was why, for most of her professional life, she avoided the recognition she craved. She was always taking classes rather than teaching them, and offering advice for free, always insisting she didn't know enough, even with her master's degree, to accept people's money. She was a compulsive gifter of her work. If someone walked into her studio, pointed at a painting, and said, "I like that," she'd tell them, "It's yours!" and then regret it later. Every few years she'd decide to overhaul. She'd hire someone to build her website, or print business cards, then fizzle out and enroll in yet another oil class. "I guess I'm just not hungry enough," she'd say, defeated. "I've never had to work for it." But she could have. Her money could have been turned around, used as a catalyst for her voice, her art.

It was something deeper that held Mary back, some fundamental reluctance to be heard. Even after Riggs and Ray and feminism, even after she'd finally named the curse, Mary's silence persisted. Where did it come from? Could it simply be chalked up to the rules all little girls of her generation had been inundated with since birth — that they should be dainty and demure, seen and not heard? Or was it something else, some indelible lesson she'd learned from Tom and his friends and, later, from Cousin John? Something about how her worth and her body were entwined and inseparable, something about how, by discarding her, they had marked her as unlovable; something about how their opinion mattered because they were men? She'd thought that Cousin John's hazy deathbed confession might free her, might allow her to go on to make a living for herself independent of his legacy, the Jell-O fortune he left behind. But instead the money worked like a cord, a binding spell, keeping her from proving, once and for all, that her voice had value.

The day she found out she was pregnant, Mary drove home, worried about how to tell George. She wasn't sure how he'd react. It didn't seem a child was in his plans;

certainly it wasn't for her. She was forty. She'd thought that door was closed. Her hands trembled, and she felt cold, then warm and sweaty. "I'm going to have a baby," she announced, standing in the doorway of the chicken coop, facing George. His hands flew to the side of his head. His hat fell off, and he hollered, scooping her up in his arms and twirling her through the air. Only then did she feel elated, only then did she allow herself to hope for wholeness and health, the child that might heal the child so damaged within her.

16

As Mary's belly grew with me inside it, George took pictures of her, pulling up her shirt to show the camera her pregnant body. The farmhouse is in the background, blue-gray and peeling; the brick path she stands on is mossy and wet. Her long, messy hair is piled on top of her head, and she is smiling shyly at my father on the other side of the lens. I imagine him teasing her gently, calling her sexy. This is how I tell myself I remember him, childlike and quick to laugh. He sang to me in my mother's belly, tender songs he made up, or the Beatles. My body knows it, remembers the muffled warmth of his voice seeping through my mother's skin, imprinting my cells and hers, painting our insides with the very best of his.

They married on a whim on a winter afternoon shortly after my birth. In the only image of the ceremony, they both wear winter coats. The dogs sit at their feet.

George has a beard and long hair; Mary wears a flower crown. They hold me, not yet one year old, in the space between them.

After my birth, my mother and I were always together. Before I could walk she wore me like an appendage in a sling across her chest. She took me with her everywhere. I was all she could talk about. She felt whole, fulfilled. The world was all sunrise. She walked in the morning light, with me strapped tight to her body, and felt newly moored. She almost forgot about the curse, all the hurdles it would present to me, all the lessons she'd have to impart. It all seemed smaller now that she was a protector, a mother-witch. Her newfound confidence began to conjure the career she'd always wanted: commissions from New Haven and New York, teaching gigs at local arts centers and private schools. In the afternoons she set me up in her studio, in a crib at first and, later, with coloring books and pencils on an old wedge of couch. She painted, and eventually so did I, the classical radio station in the background. She watched me grow and thought about Midge, dead at forty-five. She watched the sun go down outside her studio in the evenings, reflecting in shades of orange and red over the Sound, producing an upside-down image of itself in the gray water.

I always knew there was something different about my mother. Her games and stories often took dark turns before becoming light again. The world, she told me, was a dualistic place. Darkness and light fought for a balance they sometimes couldn't strike. She told me stories about what would happen when we died. How a big red pickup truck would be waiting on a sandy beach to drive us away. She set my pet goldfish free in the three-foot-deep plastic wading pool in the backyard, then marveled at their frozen corpses when winter came and the water turned to ice. At Christmas and on both our birthdays, she sent us gifts from Midge's ghost, books and big bouquets of flowers.

Maybe Mary's morbidity fed my nightmares. There was never a time when I didn't have them. Vivid scenes of witches and vampires finding me where I hid, separated from my mother, alone in the world. I'd wake in tears, muster all my courage to sneak through the hallway and to her side of the bed, where I'd shake her awake. "I had a bad dream again," I'd say, and she'd whisper *Shhh,* swing out of bed, and walk me to my room, my father grumbling and putting a pillow over his head as we left.

My mother would sit by my bedside then, rubbing my back while I told her what had happened, intricate stories of black magic more powerful than I. To this she suggested Jungian dream bargaining, in which I closed my eyes, returned to the dream, and confronted the evil I found there. "What do you want from me?" I asked the monsters that chased me. I imagined my little self, defiant and sure, a sorceress who used her power only for good. "I want to kill you," they always answered. This shook me. How should I respond? I asked Mary.

"Not an option," she would coach. "Go in and tell them they have to pick something or someone else, something in the light."

It was a lengthy exercise, too mature perhaps for a child my age. But like everything my mother taught me, the point came back to assertiveness, to the imperative that I learn, as she never had, to use my voice.

Even so, my nightmares persisted, normalizing so that in sleep I expected only darkness. The waking world, where my mother was, was where I found the light. For my whole life I felt, with her, that anything was possible. Great magic, great loss. After I started school, my mother picked me up each afternoon, a snack in the center console of her beat-up station wagon, paint under her nails, and we drove straight to West Woods, a patch of state forest full of winding trails, hidden streams. The path is wide there. It welcomed my mother and me like a road to home. The dogs ran ahead, and Mary and I held hands over the rocks. Close to her, I could smell the turpentine she painted with, a thin layer of poison under which she smelled inherently clean, like a gently soaped room, candlelit and glowing. We stopped to rest, sitting on a log, picking up leaves and twigs. We found a fort someone else had built, a shelter of branches and leaves; we made our way to my favorite place, a creek that blocked the path, falling over rocks and foaming shades of yellow and brown. The dogs would sniff around, run ahead, and return, but when it came time to leave, when we rounded the bend and saw the parking lot, my mother's dog, Lilly, would disappear. Mary called and called for her hidden dog, who stood like a statue behind the biggest tree she could find, hoping we'd decide to stay forever in the woods she loved. Over time I took to imitating her, hiding behind a tree as if frozen. But I always revealed myself to my mother, stepping out from the shadows and introducing myself to her as someone new.

"I'm Rosy," I'd say, and she would always play along, extending her hand to shake mine.

"Hi, Rosy," she'd say. "Where are your mom and dad?"

"I'm not sure," I'd tell her.

"Well, come along with me. I'll take you home." She'd smile and hold out her hand. "I've always wanted a little girl."

With Ray's help, Mary quit drinking before I was born and kept sober afterward. She liked herself better this way, she said, clear of the wash of red wine and bourbon brown she'd worn since her mother's death decades before. Here was her authentic voice, untarnished by booze. But the further into sobriety she ventured, the more my father drank.

At first it was moderate. Then it was the occasional Friday night, during which he'd stay out drinking, copping coke, which he inhaled like the lightest fragrance, the smoothest stinging scent. When he came home, dim-eyed and contrite, a tail-tucked dog braced for Mary's anger, they would argue into the night, George asking what the big fucking deal was and Mary yelling about abandonment. But they would try to forgive each other, settling back into domestic life — public television and Cherry Garcia on the couch — until the next cycle of misbehavior, argument, forgiveness. George would go out and Mary would stay up, standing at the window as if awaiting her soldier's return from war. "I developed all these nervous habits," she wrote in a letter to me once, a ritual she started when I was in college and she was sick again, "although who knows if they were really emotional or not. My stomach was a mess, and my whole body ached. My hands shook. Sometimes he'd go out, and I'd put you into the car, load up the dogs, and drive and drive, looking for somewhere safe. I'd park and sob. I'd reach over, get you out of the car seat, and hold you in my arms."

When I was three years old, George's father died, falling on the couch in his South Carolina bungalow while his heart struggled, then stopped. Several years later, Bob passed away in the dementia ward of an Arizona nursing home, leaving his wife, Ramona, alone and befuddled, dependent on an iron lung and the cinnamon sticks she plugged into her lips, pretending they were smokes.

Bob and Ramona had been my only grandparents, but they quickly faded from memory once Bob died. But when I was three and four and five, we visited them once or twice a year in their posh senior living community in Sun City. Even then, my grandfather struggled to remember the simplest things: the state he lived in, the cereal he favored, my name. My mother seemed tender with him about this, and everything. If ever she resented him for disappearing into dementia, she never showed it. When Bob truly began to die, she flew to Arizona to wait at his bedside. My father and I followed behind days later for the funeral, where there were large bouquets of white flowers and little else, a final nod to Bob's confirmed atheism.

After Bob's death, Mary began drawing up plans for her farmhouse, picking trim colors and wallpapers. I watched as men arrived in trucks to paint everything on the outside yellow, even the barn and the chicken coop behind it, where George set up his stuff: car parts and dismembered motorcycles; calendars with Jaguars and Porsches hugging tight corners; red chests of tools; a chair with wheels and a gray sheepskin cushion. The whole place smelled like oil and leather. He quit his management job with Saab, strapped on a tool belt, and became a contractor, gutting the old barn to build a studio for my mother, a spiral staircase, a fluorescent light table on which she spread slides and traced colors. Outside, the crab-apple tree dropped its fruit, ringing itself with bruised and mottled bodies. Pieces of mossy plywood were nailed into the bark, a onetime ladder going nowhere. It was, my mother said, everything she'd always dreamed of. A house in which she was contained. A studio for her art. A family. Even if all of it came from Jell-O, she chose to see it instead as coming from Midge. This was a gift, her mother to her, a reward for so many years of feeling lost, ungrounded, unsafe.

Every night in that house by the water, the Amtrak express and Shore Line East connectors blew over the salt marsh, snaking along the Long Island Sound. Mocking-birds called down the sun. In the spring, the water rose up and covered the road, swamping the front yard. George put on thigh-high waders and strode through the water, looking for important things it covered over, things he needed to find, to save.

17

The 1980s. Power women, armored in power suits, climbed the corporate ladder. Young mothers returned to school. Single mothers worked full-time to support the independence they'd won during the seventies divorce boom. Where once they'd been silenced, contained, financially dependent on marriage, now they were self-reliant, in possession of the *something more* Friedan had promised. But alongside liberation, many women discovered what underprivileged women had known for decades, and what Friedan had failed to mention: single, working motherhood was a struggle.

There was, in fact, quite a bit that Betty Friedan had failed to mention. In the decades after its publication, *The Feminine Mystique,* like the feminist wave it spurred, was taken to task for its racist and classist exclusions. In her book, Friedan had given voice only to a select and privileged population, omitting in the process the experience of the majority of American women. Soon, third wavers arrived to sardonically ask if Friedan had considered whether it was a richer emotional experience to stay at home and mother, or to enter the workforce as a prostitute or sweatshop laborer. The question became serious. Well, third wavers decided, it all depended on one's standpoint. *All* women's experiences *could be* inherently feminist. Do what you want, they argued. Wear your heels and lipstick; watch your porn, sell your body. Anything you do carries with it the potential for liberation. Even a Jell-O salad can be radical if made from a sex-positive standpoint. But Jell-O salads were last on women's list of things to make with their newfound liberation. Snacks for the road were where it was at for women under fifty, women with children: Jell-O's target audience.

Enter Jigglers, the creation of the team of MBAs tasked with finding Jell-O's next big thing. Every day for months, they gathered around a table at General Foods headquarters in New York, awaiting a new concoction by General Foods' on-site chefs. Duds abounded. Too complicated or time consuming. Too retro. But when a platter arrived bearing squares of concentrated Jell-O you could pick up and play with, the team knew they had found what they were looking for.

By the late 1980s, there were Jiggler displays in supermarkets and recipes on the backs of boxes. Jell-O sent alphabet molds to schools and sold heart-, star-, and half-moon-shaped Jiggler cutters to guilty working mothers looking for something quick and fun to do with their neglected kids. By the time Bill Cosby signed on to represent Jigglers in the early 1990s, Jell-O sales were up by 47 percent. More important, Jigglers helped Jell-O transition from dessert to snack, a change pivotal to steady profits, which increased with Jigglers, and with Cosby, whose twenty-seven-year contract with Jell-O made his the longest continuously running advertising deal between any celebrity and product.

Even so, allegations of rape and assault were constant for Cosby over the years. The stories, of which there were more than fifty, spanned decades. But it was the 2018 testimony of Andrea Constandt — with whom Cosby settled a 3.38 million-dollar lawsuit in 2006 — that resulted in a guilty verdict. As of this writing, the now eighty-year-old comedian faces up to thirty years in prison on three felony counts of aggravated indecent assault.

Following the verdict, newspapers trumpeted Cosby's trial — at which five of his alleged victims testified — as a triumph for women and a direct result of the #metoo movement. For decades, like that of so many powerful men of his ilk, Cosby's behavior had been an "open secret." But to come forward against him was particularly dangerous, the accuser risking an onslaught of victim blame and vitriol exacerbated by her tormentor's public persona. Cosby was beloved, his fan base wide and loyal. For them he triggered childhood nostalgia, home and safety and sweet, sweet Jell-O. What good was a woman's word next to all that?

In commercials from Cosby's heyday, he is equal parts daddish and infantile, flinging Jigglers with kids in one ad, then donning a Cosby sweater and reminiscing solo to the camera about his childhood in another. He is versatile, molding to consumers' needs. He is comforting in his sameness over the years. He simply wants to spread the word about light and wholesome Jell-O. He is threatening no one! He is symbolic of racial harmony in America, the square and safe black man we can all agree to love. He is the patriarchal passive nudger, guiding women back into the kitchen with a hand lightly placed on the small of their backs.

18

When I turned two, my mother began to disappear. I looked for her in her studio, in the kitchen, the garden, but found her in her bathroom, hunched over the toilet bowl, little tears in the corners of her eyes. "Hi, honey bun," she'd say, frowning and holding out her arms to me when I cried at the sight of her. "Everything's all right": a refrain. But she turned pale, grew thin. She went to doctors, one after another. "It's stress," they told her. "You're being hysterical," they said. "But look at my family history," she insisted. She brought out the paperwork from Riggs, the psychiatric evaluations. "Well, here you go," doctors told her, suggesting her symptoms were probably part of a psychotic episode. Their coincidence with her menstrual cycle made it all the more likely that she was suffering from conversion disorder, or PMS, which was itself considered a kind of hysteria. They suggested tranquilizers. "You're perfectly *physically* healthy, Ms. Fussell," they said as their pens scratched across their prescription pads. Not, it would one day turn out, unlike the girls of LeRoy, who, following doctors' visits and ER trips, were told the same thing as my mother. Anti-anxiety drugs, hormonal birth control, and pamphlets on stress relief remained, by the time the LeRoy girls sought help, twenty-four years after my mother's first symptoms, the first line of defense for doctors faced with complaints historically attributed to "female problems."

At first Mary tried to believe them. Better stress than cancer. She tried the drugs. She tried calming teas and long naps. She tried meditation, self-help books, classical music. Years passed and she remained sick. "Nothing helps," she told a new doctor, who suggested she cut wheat and yeast out of her diet. So she did. Nothing changed, and she wondered if she was imagining her illness after all, conjuring it like a shadow from her childhood, her memory of Midge, whose symptoms had arisen at this very age.

I was four when another pregnancy confirmed Mary's well-being. "Women your age don't get pregnant unless they are perfectly healthy," her doctors said. She touched her stomach and imagined a boy, my brother. She thought of Tom. And my father, whose distance had grown alongside her illness, his fear and frustration running parallel to hers; who yelled when they fought, and often: "You're being crazy." Suddenly, he was turning, changing into a volatile version of himself, exasperated by her inability to name the symptoms she experienced, the pain she felt. If George couldn't see it, it wasn't real. Especially when it came to the body, which he saw as something to ignore, to use like a tool. Later, though, after my mother's illness, he would come to see it as something to control, something to perfect through excessive exercise, the vitamins he began to take by the handful, the protein shakes he ate instead of meals.

But before all that, as Mary struggled to solve her symptoms through elimination diets, George ate. Pints of ice cream, a dinner of hot dogs, six at a time. Their bodies diverged, curled onto separate sides of the California king bed they'd bought with their new wealth. It was ironic, Mary thought, that as her inheritance paid for the bed she slept in, the house she loved, her symptoms persisted and her sanctuary by the water became yet another place in which a man she trusted insisted that she quiet down.

The day she told George she was pregnant again, he ran his hands through his hair, filled his cheeks with air, and exhaled slowly. Keeping the child was a question now. She was forty-five, Midge's age when she died.

A week later, my mother heard screaming from the backyard where my friends and I played. "Mary, Mary!" a choir of girl voices called. "Allie's stuck on the monkey bars!" She didn't hesitate. She ran. Out to the swing set where I hung, paralyzed. She held up her arms to catch me and felt in that instant the blood between her legs.

"It would have happened anyway," she told me years later, knowing what I needed to hear. "It wasn't your fault."

Two months before I turned five, my mother turned forty-six. She found a new doctor, a young woman with a thick brown ponytail who met her eyes when they spoke. This doctor listened and ran tests, and though they remained inconclusive, Mary's symptoms worsened. "Well," her doctor said, "I'd like to go in and look around." It was the very thing so many men before her had warned against: elective surgery and with nothing but the patient's word to warrant it. But it was the only way to truly know. So Mary signed the paperwork, tucked her curls into a surgical bonnet, and climbed onto a gurney. In a theater, under fluorescent lights, surgeons cut her from sternum to pelvis. They pulled feet of small intestine from her belly. I imagine them wrestling with it like a venomous snake, yellow and malignant. They counted the tumors then, the one large one, the other smaller satellites. "It would have killed you in a year," they later told her, standing in a faceless group over her bed, delivering her diagnosis. It was carcinoid, they said, sucking their chins into their necks, a rare form of cancer characterized by hormone-secreting tumors. This, they said, was the reason for her miscarriage, and for the sickness that plagued her each month, with each period, like a punishment.

The seam in Mary's stomach beat in time with her blood. She imagined that the tumors had also aligned with this rhythm, pumping venom before they'd been found and cut out, just soon enough to save her. She wanted to scream at the doctors, at her husband, to impress upon them the gravity of their mistake, the life of her little daughter who'd been nearly left alone. She had known she was sick. She'd been saying it for two years, ever since the symptoms first appeared, arriving like a prophecy when she turned forty-two, the same age Midge had been when she'd found the lump.

But how had she known? Lying alone and awake in her hospital bed, Mary thought about the legacy of illness, wondering if her fixation with Midge's early death might somehow beget her own. "In matters of health, you manifest what you imagine," one of the naturopaths she'd consulted had said, which seemed at the time ridiculous and now — Mary weak and drugged and plugged into wires, an eight-inch scar down the middle of her stomach — prophetic; her cancer a penance for so much negative thought, for the badness she'd been branded with as a child. *What's wrong with me?* she'd asked so many times in her life, and now she knew.

In truth she'd saved herself. But in the anesthetic haze, she saw only her own part in her illness, how she'd conjured it some-how, staying silent with the boys, her cousin; staying hidden when Midge had needed her the most. Later she'd learn to turn the thought around, to rage at the medical establishment instead of herself. But it never stopped trying to get through.

"The voice may be in us, but it's not us," she'd one day promise me when the same invisible meanness perched behind my ears, whispering of my inadequacy. "That's the voice of patriarchy," she'd tell me, "and it's our job to tell him to shut the fuck up. Trust me, honey bun," she'd add, "this isn't your fault." How many times did she assure me of my blamelessness? *This isn't your fault*, she'd insist, squeezing my hand, trying to shake me out of whatever hole of silent self-loathing I'd fallen down. And when the girls of LeRoy began to show symptoms, I imagine their mothers said the same, knowing, as my mother did, that their daughters lived in a culture that told them the opposite.

There is a series of photographs taken of Mary the day before her surgery. She kneels in the winter sunlight and does not smile. Her white button-down shirt is tucked neatly into the waist of her full denim skirt. She has rolled small circles of blush onto the apples of her cheeks, but the rest of her is so bloodless and thin that the makeup looks artificial. And then I am beside her, wearing my dress-up clothes and carrying a basket as if I am about to gather wildflowers. I remember little of the time surrounding this surgery, but I can recall this day and this photo shoot in some detail. Enough at least to remember that I had been excited by the premise of these pictures, the spectacle of them, and asked to pick my own outfit, selecting with care the floor-length blue dress made for an adult woman, which draped, tentlike, from my five-year-old frame. I thought it was a game, I thought it was make-believe. Cancer was as appropriately amorphous to me as, I imagine, it was to my mother when Midge fell ill. As little girls we lived in the *now,* a state my mother would one day try to reclaim. *I'm all right now!* she'd chime from hospital beds and gurneys, echoing the Eckhart Tolle self-help audiobook she listened to in her car when she was well enough to drive. By then, she'd become familiar with the realities of her illness, the nearness of her own death: the paperwork she signed before going under the knife, the long rehabilitation and painful complications when she woke.

But when I was a child and she first fell ill, she appeared shocked. For years she'd insisted there was something physically wrong with her. When it turned out there truly was, fear opened for her like a matryoshka doll, diagnoses, symptoms, and treatments nested inside one another in the shape of a shrinking woman's body, all lead-ing to a single, solid truth: her own death.

After the surgery, Mary stayed in the hospital, and without her, time stretched, and shrank, so that I couldn't decipher its passing. Days, weeks, I couldn't tell. Our family routines disappeared. My father and I ate pizza and Greek salads. We rented movies from the local Reel to Reel. He picked me up after school and took me home to a quiet house, only the dogs waiting, tails thumping, for our return. On the weekends he dropped me off at a friend's house, where her mother seemed extra gentle, extra willing to pile us into the car for frozen yogurt and mini golf.

One evening, he picked me up and kissed the top of my head when I buckled myself into the passenger seat. "Should we go see Mommy?" Excitement shot up my legs, turned to buzzing inside my stomach. *Yes, yes, let's go.* All the way to New Haven in the blue Volvo station wagon, inherited from my father's father. He held my hand, and we walked from the parking garage through a tube suspended over the street below, into the hospital. "This is where I was born," I announced proudly, as if it were news to him. My father always told me that the day of my birth was the happiest of his life. But today he was quiet, worried. He knelt down to my level before we entered my mother's room. "Try and speak softly," he said.

Inside the dim room, my mother slept. We shuffled in, and she blinked her eyes open. "Hi, honey bun," she said, her voice sticky. The bed was high, and I could barely see her, but my father lifted me up and propped me on the side. I leaned across her, desperate for a hug, a little weight landing on her stomach. She winced. "Does that hurt?" I asked, pulling away. She shook her head and smiled, rearranged me, then drew me close.

"Here," she said, handing me a small plastic cup of pink Jell-O, covered with a tinfoil lid. "A treat just for you."

In a week she was home and set up on the couch. In a month she was walking and painting again. A synagogue in New Haven commissioned four walls' worth of stained-glass windows — the story of Moses from start to finish — and she threw herself into designing them. But she wanted to get back to nature, wanted the quiet of the woods, the patter of raindrops on the roof of a tent in which she slept, safe and warm.

She finished the windows in the early spring, receiving the check for her work like an emblem of her value. With it she bought a powder-blue tent for three, a Coleman stove, three brown sleeping bags, and an old rust-spotted Suburban. She swung the truck doors open and stood out in the driveway and packed for days, filling the cavernous truck from floor to ceiling. When school let out, we left, my father behind the wheel, my mother looking out the passenger-side window, and me buckled onto the bench-style front seat, in between the two of them.

My mother still placed her palms over her stomach then, still slept in the afternoons, her head drooping into the seatbelt. My father listened to tapes, mouthing the words, patting the steering wheel softly, keeping time, keeping his eyes on the road. We camped from Connecticut to Idaho, stopping from time to time at a hotel, where I'd flounder around in the swimming pool and my parents would shower and brush their wet hair, my mother's curls separated by plastic teeth, transformed into smooth, wet grooves.

My parents had arranged a whole backseat world in the Suburban for me. A hammock slung along the window housed my favorite stuffed animals; a box below it held my books. They'd imagined me reading and singing and playing in the backseat while they drove, the way I had in my bedroom at home before the surgery. But I rarely did. My mother's side was where I stayed. She would angle herself next to the window and prop her feet up on the dashboard, and I would fit myself into the hinge of her armpit. She would nap, my father would turn up the CB radio he'd bought before the trip, and we'd listen to the truckers talking shop and comparing routes. Once, a disembodied voice from the Chiquita banana truck we kept passing complimented my mother's legs, her slender feet, with such persistence that my father reached over and woke her up. She blushed, took her feet off the dash. My father always said my mother had racehorse legs. He said this playfully, but this time he seemed more angry than proud. In truth he seemed this way for much of the trip, constantly aggravated, like he had swallowed his guilt for not believing her and it had turned sour in his gut. When they spoke, he struggled to find words, as if he were trying to speak a language only my mother knew, as if he were trying to decipher how she spoke her despair.

There are several photographs — taken by me, I suppose — of my parents fighting that summer, our campsite behind them, the Rocky Mountains strung across the skyline like jagged teeth. My father has his arms spread open, his elbows bent. His palms face the sky, and his shoulders shrug as if he is asking, *What do you want from me?* I wonder now if he was simply angered by what he couldn't see, tumors and fears.

That autumn, we returned, and Mary began to write her memoir, a bid for her own sanity that she would ultimately leave unfinished. She told me in desperation how much she needed to write herself down. I didn't know it then, but her work would become a kind of spell book for me, a story I'd consult, looking for the answers to illness and loss.

At first, the book grew with urgency. Piles of pages cropped up around my mother's desk, her body, which swayed, trance-like, while she wrote. Sometimes it stilled itself and she read, her forehead creased into a look of concern. The book became her job, her obsession. She began every morning, a cup of coffee separating from its cream, forgotten on the desk beside her, and worked through the afternoon, into the evening. She was always late to the dinner table, always asking for just one more word. When my father bought her a computer, she learned to type in a practiced pattern dictated by a chart she kept posted above her desk, and churned out pages with a mechanical rapidity. "There is this stream inside," she told me, "there is this current." It runs like blood, but it beats to be released.

"Tell me again what you're writing about," I'd often ask when she first began, the answer still novel. I was six years old and wondering where my mother was, wondering what story had absented her from ours. "I'm writing the story of my life," she'd say, not yet ready to explain she was writing about the curse she felt, always hanging over her, a gloaming. If I pressed, she'd tell me about Jell-O, LeRoy, and Riggs. Years later, when she was still writing and I was old enough to read her work, the stories from Riggs read familiarly, as if they were mine as well. But the workshop groups she attended told her the book was muddled and unclear. "This is pointless," she'd say, pulling her forehead through her hands, a gesture of surrender.

But she never gave up for long. When Susanna Kaysen's *Girl, Interrupted* came out to glowing reviews, she said, "She beat me to it," as if her story had been stolen. For a week she stayed away from the studio, paying bills at the kitchen table and gardening, hunched over and frowning into her neglected flower beds. She went to therapy, talked to her friends, then cut out a review of Kaysen's book, taped it to the beam above her desk, and kept writing. She bought books on agents and publishers. Letters went out, rejections came back. She joined more workshops, came home upset and angry. And still, over the years, she kept writing. She wrote as we packed boxes, moved everything from the dream house on the water to a house in the woods of New Hampshire — dark brown where the other had been yellow, A-framed and isolated, set off the road by a long, winding driveway full of ruts. In her new office she wrote, surrounded by unpacked boxes. I tried to accompany her as she worked, as I had in her Connecticut studio, curled on a cushion in the afternoon sun. But the light was harder to find in this new house, which was always cold, the sun always sinking behind it, enveloped by the surrounding woods too early in the day, so that darkness always seemed to be falling.

In years to come, my mother and I would look back on the house and wonder how we didn't know. How did we not see the place for what it was? Cold and dark, hundreds of miles from the water and from West Woods, the path we loved, this new house was an echo chamber for our three voices: my father's short and distant, my mother's high and pleading, and mine slowly falling silent in the space between them.

As years passed in the New Hampshire house, my parents' fights became more frequent, their strained voices seeping through the floorboards that separated their room from mine, an anxious lullaby I'd later find it hard to sleep without. They raged at night. In the mornings, they'd be quiet, working around each other, around me, each one off to their separate home office. By this time my mother had been working on her memoir for several years. But she was, she sighed, no closer to an end point. My father, who'd once proudly proclaimed that Mary would soon be promoting her book on *Oprah,* now held up a story I'd written in my fourth-grade English class, scoffing, "Allie will probably be the first published author in this family."

Once my father had called my mother's art "genius" and built her a studio to house it. But the longer we stayed in the New Hampshire house, the more disdainful he became of her, and the more I, too, began to think of her as self-indulgent, what my father called "high maintenance." *What does she think is so special about her life?* I would ask, the first hints of exasperated adolescence thickening my voice. She'd purse her lips, affronted, and return to her work. I was supposed to *know* the answer.

What I think I know now, what I think she meant then but couldn't yet say, was that my mother hoped her life might serve as a warning to other women, including me. Mary's mother loss and illness, her fear of being labeled hysterical and her willingness to believe it when she was, had silenced her throughout her life. In writing her memoir she was reclaiming her voice, even as she failed to notice that I was losing mine. But she was obsessed, blinded by an imperative to keep speaking and to stave off sickness. Patriarchy and its cursed mandates had performed itself through her doctors, all of them conspiring to keep her quiet, and now she was going to write a spell to keep cancer away, her work a message to other women that they should do the same.

19

In 1995, Jell-O sales got a boost from Jiggler Eggs, debuted for Easter and featured
at the White House egg roll. In 1996, when
astronaut Shannon Lucid embarked on a
140-day mission to the Russian space station, *Mir,* where she would serve as the
station's first female astronaut, she brought
powdered Jell-O packed in drinking bags.
Lucid ate her Jell-O only on Sundays, to
remind herself of home and to keep track of
the days until her return. This was, and
perhaps always has been, Jell-O in a nut-
shell: an emblem of home, a keeper of time,
equal parts powder and water, nostalgia and
modernity.

By the time Jell-O's hundredth anniversary
arrived, in 1997, the product's identity was
leaning more toward adulthood than childhood. The sugar-free products popular with
dieters accounted for 40 percent of Jell-O's

sales. The introduction of a limited-edition Sparkling White Grape flavor — rolled out in celebration of a hundred years of Jell-O, and so popular it became permanently available — necessitated club soda to make and replicated a sort of congealed champagne. It was served in fancy flutes at a birthday gala thrown by Kraft (which had merged with General Foods in 1990) at Cooper Union, and was accompanied by a new catchphrase: *Jell-O Always Breaks the Mold.*

In LeRoy, Sparkling White Grape was unveiled at the annual Oatka Festival, known best for a rubber ducky race across Oatka Creek. In 1997, however, the Oatka Festival showcased not only a new Jell-O flavor but a new Jell-O gallery, the brainchild of LeRoy town historian Lynne Belluscio. Once a narrow hallway exhibit at Strong Memorial Hospital in Rochester, with funding from Kraft, the Jell-O Gallery took up residence in the old LeRoy high school, transforming the space into a mix of children's museum and serious documentation of Jell-O's origin, manufacture, and marketing.

Mary had always been hesitant about Jell-O, rarely keeping it in the house, rarely talking about our connection to it, how it supported our life. She had been hesitant, too, about the curse. She didn't want me to believe I was at a disadvantage because I was a girl. She didn't want to scare me. And maybe that's why we stayed away from LeRoy the way we did, visiting only a few times when I was a baby. But she must have thought a hundred years of Jell-O was her chance to gently show me something about where I came from and what to avoid. Maybe she assumed I'd see in LeRoy, with its pristine and perfect small-town image, the patriarchal stronghold she saw. Maybe she assumed I'd understand the curse through osmosis. She was wrong. Whereas Mary always said she could *feel* the town's dark underbelly, unhealthy beneath its sweet exterior, I felt safe there. Or I thought I did. Thinking of it now, I wonder if I felt safe in LeRoy or if I simply felt safe with my mother, wherever we were.

The day before the celebration, we drove in on Main Street, making our way to the east side of town, where the trees cast shadows, wide and flecked with light. In the cemetery we found Midge's and Bob's headstones, tucked like ornaments into the bright-green grass. They were so small and unimposing, enveloped by the earth. Soft moss crept quietly over the etched name and date of Midge's older headstone, erasing her entirely. "Oh," my mother said as she kneeled before her mother's grave, placing her hands firmly into the soil as if she might sink in if she pressed hard enough. I trotted around, gathering sticks, and together we scraped the moss away.

As we worked, I pressed for stories about my grandmother. My mother often told me tales that began *When I was a little girl,* and these were my favorite. I wanted to know what she was like when she was my age; she wanted to talk about her mother. Talking about Midge had become, in the years directly before and after my birth, an obsession for Mary. For most of her life, she'd been ruled by guilt, the image of herself crouched cowardly behind the shed, unable or unwilling to save her mother; and by the image of Midge as distant and diseased, the *bad mother* whose decomposing body haunted her nightmares, a punishment. But with Ray, she'd learned to rewrite the story, to cast Midge in the light, to forgive her for her distance, and for leaving her only daughter alone too soon. So the grandmother I learned of was forgiving and saintly, the *elegant white goddess* my mother wrote her as. It was only when I became a woman myself that I returned to Midge's letters, interpreting in her careful prose hints of her true feelings about motherhood, the ways in which she felt rent apart by the responsibility of it, the way she loved her children even as she felt they'd torn from her the life she could have had.

That night my mother sat on the side of my bed in Tom's guest room, telling me stories about my family. Orator and Pearle Wait, signing the Jell-O contract. The rainbow-colored river. Holidays at Uncle Ernest and Aunt Edith's mansion, Edith summoning servants carrying glittering Jell-O molds by touching her toe to a button hidden beneath the table. At first her stories were light! and dainty! But as she went on, I sensed a familiar darkness there, behind her words. She talked about Mr. Wait's misfortune, how he died impoverished, forever sorry he had sold his best invention. She talked about the frightened animals who spent their lives in cages before their bones became Jell-O. She held my hand. My eyelids fluttered, chasing sleep. "There's always a dark side to the light," she told me. "The dark, it chases us especially, and we need to be careful."

"Why?" I asked her, waking up now.

"Well," she said, "there's a curse, and though it's everywhere, it's particularly strong in our family, in Jell-O and in Le-Roy."

"What's the curse?" I asked her.

"I've spent most of my life trying to figure that out." She sighed. "Growing up I learned it was money. Now I think it's silence, and the sickness silence plants, like seeds, inside women." As she spoke, she mimed planting seeds with her fingertips along the thin line of my forearm.

"Is that what made my grandmother sick?" I asked.

"Probably," she answered.

"Is that what made you sick?"

"Yes," she said.

"But how does Jell-O make women silent?" I asked, entirely confused.

"By convincing us we're less powerful than we really are," she told me. "That's why I need to write. That's why I need to tell the world about my life. I need to break the silence."

20

If my mother were to warn the world about the curse, I would help her. I would write, too. So when we returned from LeRoy and I turned eleven, my father set up a table for me in my New Hampshire bedroom, with a desk lamp and a container for my pencils and pens, my paper clips and highlighters. But the room stayed dark, shaded by the woods that began outside my bedroom window, a front of tall trees stretching on for acres. They were beautiful, the trees, their long trunks gathered, but something about their nearness, the edge of the dark world their bodies shaped so close to the light childhood world I still lived in, always felt like a warning to me. Like so many of my nightmares, I ignored it.

Another year passed. I turned twelve. My body toed the waters of womanhood while my mother wrote. I lay on my belly by her feet and wrote as well. Downstairs, my father was in his home office, investing money he'd inherited from his father, a hobby turned occupation. He earned some, enough to buy himself a fancy car and skis and running shoes, but it only supplemented Mary's Jell-O money. Maybe this made my father feel trapped, this financial dependence on his wife. It seemed he was always running from something. Running was his escape, he said. He needed it. He needed to keep his body conditioned, lean and trim and flexible, an inhospitable environment for disease. He subscribed to a magazine called *Life Extension* and ordered supplements he swallowed by the handful. He spoke with disgust of the way he used to eat as he loaded the blender with protein powder, preparing to run, as he did every evening, up and down the country roads, wearing fractures into the arches of his feet. This was when he was happiest.

The director of my eighth-grade musical seemed to take a special interest in me, her star performer. For weeks before opening night, she marked out with masking tape the pivots for me to make as I walked across the stage. She stood at the back of the auditorium with her arms folded and called out, "Louder!" She cinched the waist of my costume, fitting her cold fingertips into the creases made by my belt and skirt, smoothing out the fabric and tucking a pink heart-shaped stone into the waistband. "For good luck," she said. When I climbed into my father's car at the end of the day, I found a matching crystal in the cup holder.

I didn't say anything. Not even after I found a pair of black panties in the laundry, definitively not my mother's. But it all unraveled quickly anyway. My father's affair, my mother's betrayal. She'd walked in on them, she said. "He was unzipping her fucking dress," she told me, spitting her words, her tone so violent I cowered in my seat. I closed my eyes against my tears and pressed my body into the door, as far away from her, as far away from the truth she spoke, as I could get. She said nothing as I rocked back and forth, just put a hand on my shoulder. But I recoiled from her touch, the nearness of her skin calling me back to my own, which ached. All I knew was that I needed to escape this ache. All I knew was that I needed to disappear.

In the small community of my middle school, gossip ran rampant. Before long, everyone was whispering about my parents, the drama teacher, and me. My mother blushed bright red when she dropped me off at school. She bought a pair of sunglasses — which she normally never wore — to hide behind. She looked so diminished, her face masked by dark moons, and for the first time in my life, I wondered if she was strong enough to bear her pain.

About all this my father said nothing. So finally I mustered the courage to ask him: had he really cheated on Mom, like everyone was saying? In response he slammed his palms on the steering wheel. "Your mother's hysterical," he warned, while I disappeared into the passenger seat beside him, imagining myself blending in with the upholstery, camouflaged like prey. Afterward, he fell silent again and stayed that way. Even as my mother moved her things from the New Hampshire house, curls bouncing as she bent beneath the weight of boxes, he pursed his lips, storing up anger to unloose later, over something benign — the sleeping dog he tripped over on his way to the kitchen, the lamp left lit after I left a room. *Jesus Christ!* he'd scream, a man unhinged. His rage terrified me. But his silence was worse. In it I could sense him brewing a winter storm, gray clouds growing heavy before unloading a whiteout and erasing the world.

227

My parents would split custody, it was decided. This was the humane way to handle one element of a divorce that was quickly turning into a battle. *Please don't leave me,* I wanted to beg my mother. Without her, the New Hampshire house became a sinkhole, dangerous and dark, a bottomless pit of empty time, threatening to consume me. How would I spend my afternoons without my mother there to write with? Who would I talk to? Who would I hide behind when my father was upset?

My mother's removal from the New Hampshire house put me in my father's line of fire. So I learned to stay silent and small. I learned to side with him, to assume his version of reality rather than suffer the repercussions of contesting it. I got so good at playing the role of my father's perfect daughter, perfect sidekick, perfect secret keeper, that I forgot how to be anything else. I maintained his version of reality for the sake of self-preservation, but I did so with a vehemence that, eventually, made me question reality itself.

My dark-green room became for the first time a sanctuary, and I spent most of my time sprawled out on the floor, listening to music and writing in my journal, the carpet pressing scratchy impressions into the skin of my thighs, which were suddenly hideous to me. I stared at them constantly. It was as if I'd awoken one day to a world in which I was fat and ugly and unwanted. How could I have missed this before? How could I not have known to be vigilant? I pushed and pulled at the skin, trying to arrange it to appear lean and diminished, like that of the girls on the pages of my *Seventeen* magazines. I wanted everything about the girls: their concave legs and straight hair, their flat chests and innocence. I bought bras to squash my incoming breasts, then practiced an apathetic slump, the waifish posture of the thin and hungry. I was thirteen, about to graduate from the eighth grade. My body was a transformative object, changing from child to woman, a conversion I understood as burdensome. With maturity, I realized, thinking of my mother, came the promise of pain. But if I could stop it, if I could arrest my own development, maybe I could return to being the girl I had been before the affair, the divorce, and the unbearable weight of the grief I now wore like an injured body, draped over my shoulders.

Every morning my father made me a

heaping bowl of oatmeal I tried to chew but could hardly swallow. He made eggs then, huge mounds of yellow scramble topped with cheese. But questions caught in my throat — *Why wasn't she good enough?* — and, unable to ask them, I couldn't swallow. All I could think of was the drama teacher, the smallness of her body, how she never seemed to consume, her appetite satiated by her own perfection. On some level I knew my efforts to stop time and stay a child were futile. But if I had to become a woman, I decided, I wanted to be a woman like my drama teacher, a woman my father approved of. I could see how painful the alternative was.

Across the river, in her new house in Vermont, Mary started Weight Watchers. Each night she added up points on Post-it notes she stuck to the cupboards, the fridge, until the glue gave out and they fell, yellow squares fluttering to the floor like leaves. "I really think you should try to stay with this," I said anytime she complained, assuming my father's exasperated voice, running my eyes from her toes to the top of her head like a disparaging man. My mother's failure to diet right, to control herself, was suddenly disgusting to me. I wanted her to talk back to me, to reclaim her body and the strength that had seeped from her since my father's affair, leaving her pale and tired, unable to fight the curse. But she couldn't, and in her silence, the curse whispered to me, urging me to show my mother how to restrict herself, how to make the sacrifices necessary to become desirable. So I joined Weight Watchers, too, and points became all that mattered; they gave our world order. We made sugar-free Jell-O together, preparing big vats of raspberry and grape we kept in the fridge, a "safe" food we could eat with abandon, the faintly metallic taste dissolving on our tongues. Sometimes Mary made a face when she spooned it in like medicine.

"It's really not good," she'd say, still eating.

"Don't eat it, then," I'd snap, annoyed.

"But I'm so hungry," she'd say, like an admonished child.

Most nights we sat together at the kitchen table, a bowl of wobbly pink in the space between us, spooning it into our mouths as we tallied up the day's intake. I always beat her. The game, for me, was easy. When she dropped out, I continued. I felt victorious. I felt I had somehow won proof of whatever it was that would spare me her fate, imperfect and discarded by my father, a man, whose gaze defined us both.

The ground was always threatening to crack and open like a wound. Someone could always get sick, someone could always lie and leave. I feared catastrophe, and so I counted, ordering the world with numbers. Calories and clock hands, pounds of body weight, the hours between meals, the hours before sleep, which I induced with pills stolen from my mother's cabinet — the only way to free myself from the nightmares that plagued me. I fixated on numbers, and I fixated on the drama teacher's body, the way she baby-oiled it so that her skin shone sun-kissed and sleek. I thought of this as I oiled my own, fresh skin. I thought of the places where she was aging and pillowy while I ran hands over myself, making notes on what I liked, what I disliked, what I wanted. I imagined cataloging the woman in the same detail, counting her freckles, noting dark roots or that particular sweep of her thin hair through the headband of her sunglasses, perched atop her head. I matched myself against her, against my mother. I already knew the woman was the better one. But I could best her, I decided; I could make myself desirable and different, the woman so perfect no man would ever leave.

In the end I felt I'd won.

The drama teacher started coming around. "We're just friends," my father maintained, always telling me reality was different from the scene before my eyes. But she cried like a jilted lover on the couch one night when she showed up unannounced at his house. Too much white wine, too many painkillers, I suspected, thinking I recognized her particular brand of fallen apart. I remember her holding on to the sleeves of my sweatshirt, pulling at them, talking about my father's anger.

"Sometimes," she said, "sometimes he's just so mean."

I nodded. "You have to stand up to him," I said, and she told me she couldn't, not the way I could.

"Because he loves you so much," she said. "How can I make him love me so much?"

My father had thrown up his hands and left her there with me, even though her presence always made me fluttery, my hands shaking, my heart palpitating in my head. When he returned, it was to carry her to the car while she punched at him, screaming, *"No, I want to stay!"* He drove her home, thirty minutes away in the blinding snow that night.

When I mentioned her episode the next morning and said I wanted to talk about it, my father told me there was nothing to say. "It's in the past," he said, his voice thickening with the promise of rage. "You need to get past this." This was what he always said. To press him only made him mad. So I stopped talking about any of it, stopped talking entirely, stopped crying. I feared that if I allowed even a single tear to fall, I wouldn't be able to stanch the deluge that would follow. And I knew what would happen then. I imagined my father's house, flooded with my tears, and him standing by, dry and impervious, calling me hysterical, the label he'd given my mother. The label, eventually, he gave the drama teacher, too. I knew, like them, I would become unlovable.

21

Our month on Weight Watchers was the only time my mother and I made Jell-O together. But there was plenty of low-point Jell-O to be made. Weight Watchers recipe books and blogs teem with "safe" dessert recipes. Whole websites still exist, lauding the utility of sugar-free Jell-O for the modern dieter. But America's obsession with calories (a term coined in the late 1800s, just before Jell-O itself was created) started in the late 1970s, gaining traction throughout the eighties and nineties, when diet plans predicated on restricting or counting calories proliferated. The idea that all food was created equal, that a calorie is a calorie, be it from broccoli or beer, reigned supreme and remains the basis for modern programs. In the late 1960s, low-fat cottage cheese and cantaloupe arrived on many American menus, and green salads made a comeback, particularly among women, who were under cultural pressure to stay young and thin, a pressure that seemed to grow with each stride they made toward equality.

Around this time Jean Nidetch, a homemaker from Queens, frustrated by her inability to lose the excess forty pounds she'd gained as a newlywed, began holding impromptu meetings in her living room. Once a week Nidetch and her friends gathered to chat about their diet programs, share tips, and bemoan failures. From these meetings, Weight Watchers was born. The plan was simple, based in part on a diet developed by the New York City Bureau of Health, where Nidetch was a patient at the obesity clinic before striking out on her own. Whereas in decades to come, Weight Watchers would be known for its trademarked "points system," at the outset it consisted more of practical recipes and lengthy lists of food to be avoided.

It was onto the "forbidden list" that original Jell-O was placed, perhaps because in the process of containing and masking ingredients, it also added "empty" calories from sugar. As if in rebuttal, an entire chapter of *The New Joys of Jell-O,* published in 1974, is devoted to "Salads for the Slim Life," all of which clock in at under 350 calories and come with considerate serving suggestions for those who value keeping fit. The molded ham and egg salad, for example, could be served over a bed of Boston lettuce with two slices of tomato and a cup of chicken broth, should diners wish to confine lunch to the 350-calorie mark. The jellied turkey salad should be paired with romaine lettuce, a quarter cup of cottage cheese, two green pepper strips, five thin carrot sticks, and a teaspoon of low-cal French dressing, all of which adds up to exactly 235 calories.

Nidetch's Weight Watchers concept arrived at an opportune moment for Americans recovering from the economic glut of the 1950s and '60s. The country was entering a transformational time, and American women followed suit. Nidetch was a prime example; by the time she sold Weight Watchers to Heinz in 1978, her body, not just her bank account, had undergone a conversion. She'd lost forty pounds and changed her hair from a modest brown bob to an elaborate blond bouffant. It was at Heinz that the Weight Watchers program changed as well, overhauling the old recipes and instating the point-based "exchange program" for which the franchise is known today.

Jell-O had worked long and hard to associate itself with the dietary needs of house-wives and nuclear families. But in the midst of second-wave feminism and the divorce boom of the seventies, Jell-O seemed a throwback to an era women in particular were eager to forget. Although older women continued to buy it, the younger women who represented the bulk of America's buying power did not. Add to that the discovery of Jell-O shots and Jell-O wrestling by fraternity brothers across America, and the dessert was suddenly tainted, considered less wholesome by its target market.

Though sales picked up with the arrival of Bill Cosby in 1974, and the advent of the pudding pops he peddled to kids, it was the diet craze of the mid-eighties that really allowed Jell-O to make a comeback with its original audience: women. Sugar-free Jell-O, containing NutraSweet, arrived on the scene in 1984 as a replacement for D-Zerta, a product that had never really taken off, due in part to its artificial taste but also public distrust of the saccharin it was made with, an additive linked to blood-borne cancers and associated with serious health concerns. Although also associated by some with an array of illnesses, NutraSweet has somehow escaped the public's wariness of its sac-charin cousin. Sugar-free Jell-O is now considered a Weight Watchers zero-points-plus food, so safe that you can eat a whole bucketful and not feel guilty.

"My childhood loves were dessert and Tommy," a permed brunette tells the camera trained on her face. She speaks as if confessing something personal, a secret she wants to keep between the two of us. The camera stays close as she lifts a spoon to her mouth, letting it linger before lusciously pulling it away. "I got over Tommy," she says, smirking, "but I *still* love dessert." The next shot is of a blue box with red lettering, JELL-O. "Eight-calorie sugar-free Jell-O gelatin," the woman's disembodied voice says, "the dessert you don't have to desert." Cut back to her, her whole body this time, tall and thin in skin-tight jeans. "Eat your *heart* out, Tommy," she says, making eye contact with her audience before spooning in another bite.

Oh, what a dream. To eat what we most desire and still be desired by Tommy. To eat as if it doesn't count. This in particular was an adolescent fantasy for me. Sometimes I'd ask myself, *If I could eat anything and not have it count, what would it be?* Plates and plates of pancakes, perhaps; a whole pizza topped in fried eggplant and sprinkled with black olives; a dripping bacon cheeseburger with all the fries. Or the entire birthday cake my mother dreamed of. She finally ate it, not long after she left my dad, not long before Weight Watchers, backed up against the kitchen counter in tears, steering fat forkfuls of carrot cake into her mouth as if they didn't count, as if they wouldn't be followed the next morning with guilt that weighed a body's worth.

Luckily for my mother, there was sugar-free Jell-O. Luckily for all women, advertise-ments suggested. Just eight calories a cup and zero — count that — *zero* Weight Watchers points. And what's more, eating sugar-free Jell-O will aid in your never-ending quest to win back the man who left you. "Hey, Danny," a jilted pudding fan says in another late-eighties commercial, nod-ding at the mirror as if speaking to herself, "here's one figure you miscalculated."

22

In college I could forget. My mother, my father, and the drama teacher were far away, distant like old nightmares, faded in the light. Mary was in Connecticut, busy setting herself up in an old house — the site of many holidays and parties during my childhood — still owned by Judy, who now lived part-time in Florida. My father was on the mountain in New Hampshire, eating chili in his winter coat. And I was in New York, safely contained by my small, warm dorm room strung with twinkle lights. Each night I fell asleep on a skinny mattress, counting the hours of sleep I would get, counting the yellow orbs blurring into darkness above me.

I'd chosen New York for the independence it might give me. I'd imagined myself free from the small world New Hampshire and Vermont had confined me to, and I hoped the big city might cure me of what was now becoming a serious problem. Weight Watchers had turned into an obsession; I'd traded points for calories, compulsive rituals, and a preoccupation with "safe" foods like fat-free yogurt and sugar-free Jell-O. I counted up the empty plastic containers, once filled with chemical lightness, and stacked them by the sink, a reminder of what I filled my body with. I heated up Lean Cuisine and Smart Ones dinners, standing in front of the microwave and counting the seconds until the bell rang. I sat in front of my steaming food, eyes on the clock, waiting for the minute hand to tick its way toward the hour at which I'd previously decided I could eat. Interruption of this ritual, loss of my count, rose up in my body like all the anger I'd never exorcised. Anger at my father for lying — for forcing me to accept his lies; and anger at my mother for leaving me alone in the cold New Hampshire house with my rageful dad.

My mother was angry, too. Each time she caught me in front of the microwave, or cutting my food into minuscule bites I arranged on my plate, easily countable, she slammed her palms down on the table or countertop. "This needs to stop!" she yelled, her voice thinner than normal, terrified by my shrinking body. But her fear seemed nothing in comparison with mine. She knew little of what I lived with. My father, dark and unpredictable, the voice inside my head, punishing and mean. So I'd fend her off with the language of my oppressors. "What are you talking about?" I'd yell, calling her crazy, assuming my father's stance: denial.

But deep down I knew she was right. By my junior year of high school I knew it wasn't normal to fill my journals with calories instead of dreams or crushes or fears. Even my on-again, off-again boyfriend barely made the pages. I knew this was odd. And I knew it was odd to tally each bite I took, counting every hour, the hours until my next meal, *one two three four five six*. I berated myself for my abnormality at the same time I felt I needed these rituals. Their performance was like a spell to me, and I needed it to keep myself safe.

Food and the scaffolding I built around its consumption had become a way of enabling the silence my father had forced me into with his rage, his refusal to acknowledge his affair. Any time I questioned him about anything at all, he exploded in anger or, worse, fell silent and said nothing for days. He froze me out. He gaslighted me, maintaining that my mother was hysterical even as he brought the drama teacher over for white wine and shrimp cocktail. Unable to tell what was real, I leaned on numbers — points and calories, seconds and minutes and hours of time — to structure my world.

Once I got to college, I reasoned, I could free myself from my parents and the space between their truths, and I could begin to get better. I pictured myself a New York girl, laughing with my friends at mimosa brunches. I imagined *ordering in.* I fantasized about meeting the boy who would magically free me from my own compulsive curse. In my mind he greeted me at the threshold of an apartment we shared, warm and well lit, and slipped my mental illness from my shoulders, as if undressing me in preparation for a long, safe sleep.

I wasn't ready for him. I was eighteen, saddled with a coping mechanism I still needed. But I still looked for him everywhere. In classes. In the dining hall, where I plucked my safe foods over and over from the plethora of options. I looked for him in bars, the lines to nightclubs. *Maybe this one,* I thought with each boy I met, each boy I slept with, looking for approval. It's not a unique story, how I sought to disprove my father's lessons about the source of a woman's worth in an array of boys too young to do anything but confirm them.

What felt unique, or what feels unique now, a decade later, is how internally I experienced my father's rage, my mother's self-doubt. It seemed the sight of me produced in Mary an anxious fear that she couldn't break through long enough to help me. But somewhere inside, hidden even from myself, I longed for her help, I longed for her to hold me, brush my hair off my forehead, and call me her little girl. Any time she tried, I jerked away from her touch, afraid of the feelings I knew she'd pull from me if I let her. But deep down I wanted her to force me, to hold me tight and squeeze from my miserable body the tears I couldn't shed. Even then, even as I stopped crying, stopped eating, stopped speaking, I knew there was a sadness that lived inside me, knocking on the walls of my insides, asking to be freed. But there wasn't room, I reasoned. My parents' emotions had also taken up residence inside my body, pulsing to be heard. Even the drama teacher herself had nestled in beneath my solar plexus, right next to each boy I slept with and never saw again, all of them whispering reasons to keep counting, keep starving, keep silently searching. My best had to be better, they whispered, I had to control myself and my surroundings, if I were to avoid my mother's discarded fate.

It was winter — December or January — when my hand froze. I was out with friends, all of us dancing, when I ran into a boy I knew vaguely from philosophy class. He was tan, with eyes that bugged from his face and nothing much to say. I can still picture his dim outline, the striped polo shirts he wore, the way he meant nothing to me. The way I knew in the moment that he was a new low. Because with him I was no longer searching for the boy who might save me; I was simply looking to feel wanted, even though I could tell his desire was situational, fleeting.

His apartment in a high-rise on Union Square looked out on the side of a brick building. On it, a Godzilla-big billboard for Bacardi and cola had been painted, and the thin Afroed spokesman and his mustachioed sidekick raised their glasses to me as I looked out the window, the boy's hands fluttering hungrily around my waist, fiddling with the zipper on my jeans. My mouth tasted dirty and dry. I wanted to be wanted. I wanted to leave.

I went through the motions. I watched myself move, flopping like a doll from window to unmade bed. The comforter was cheap and red. The sheets were black. The boy played with my panties, rubbing them between his fingers, feeling their scratch, their stick. His dick felt like a child's through the cotton of his boxers. I didn't want to see it. "Take these off," he ordered, tugging at my panties. The slur of his voice, demanding and infantile, told me I would never take them off, not for him. So I flipped over and straddled him, pulling his pants down around his ankles, pulling his boxers down and closing my eyes. I wrapped my lips around his cock, and he thrust it into the back of my throat, punching my gag reflex until he came and I spit sour jizz, let it dribble out of my mouth and down my chin, let it cake into my hair, so that when I woke up a few hours later, naked and spinning, I felt like I'd been cast and set, like plaster.

Was it then that I noticed my hand? Or had I dimly recognized its vibrating numbness before, figuring it'd be gone in the morning, that with the light it would dissolve? Was I too busy figuring out why I was naked, if in my sleep I'd stripped myself or if in my sleep I'd been stripped? At the time, it barely mattered. I rolled off the bed. I opened and closed my mouth, placing my few unfrozen fingers at the hinge of my jaw to feel its connection. The skin over the bone radiated numbness, like it was dripping off my cheek and slurring toward my shoulder. But it wasn't. In the boy's bathroom mirror, flecked with toothpaste and short, stubbly hairs, I examined myself, raccoon-eyed and crusty. Everything was in its rightful place. But my fingers had to be forced open, my jaw continually jiggled. I tiptoed back into the bedroom. The boy was sprawled on his back with his dick out, his head jerked to the side, his mouth open. I plucked my things from the floor, pulling my jeans back on with one hand, the light slanting through the window blinds, the Bacardi banner outside toasting the rising sun.

I walked home, disappointed and self-punishing. What had I expected? Shouldn't I know by now how unlovable I was? My body hummed with it, the whispered truth beneath the rituals I performed to make myself feel safe. It hummed with the disappointment of that boy's dick slapping my face, hitting the back of my throat, stifling and mean.

Months later I saw him standing outside a

bar with a clot of guys, all polo shirted and cologned. I was carrying groceries, teetering along in heels, yellow bags of fat-free yogurt and Jell-O digging ruts into my bent fingers. The boy looked at me and turned away and whispered to a friend, who leaned closer. The rest huddled in. I flipped my hair and walked by, looking straight ahead, thinking, *Fuckholes,* blinking tears. By then my hand had frozen other times, blurred into a claw. Sometimes my face followed suit and I thought I was having a stroke. I didn't know this had happened to my mother, too, not until I read her *memwah* a decade later. Nor did I ever consider doing anything about it. It made sense, I reasoned, that my body would fuck up, that I would fuck it up. I knew perfection on the outside took its toll within. I knew the spells I relied on to keep myself safe for now would kill me in the long run. It wasn't just the calorie restriction, the counting: I blew chemicals up my nose almost nightly by then, I filled my lungs with smoke. I pictured the clove cigarettes I bought from the corner market, thin and fragrant in their black-and-gold box, puncturing holes in my heart.

That spring, during my freshman year of college, Mary's cancer returned. Carcinoids metastasized in her liver, secreting hormones that made her blood pressure spike, her heart skip beats, her bowels dissolve into diarrhea. She made folders of CT scans and bloodwork and organized her care after the surgery, which she scheduled for later that spring.

I was calling my father nightly then to keep on his good side, and told him about the surgery from my usual perch in the stairwell of my dorm. At first he was silent, and my brain raced, trying to figure out how this would go. Would he be supportive? Angry? Or would he shut down, shut me out, become punishing and cold?

"I'd like to come," he finally said, his voice sullen and soft. "I'd like to be there to support you."

"Sure," I said lightly. But inside I was panicking. I knew my mother wouldn't like this, and I couldn't say no to my dad.

"Absolutely not," Mary said when I emailed her about it. "I do not want him there." She had already organized a posse of her friends to wait with me. These people were, she reminded me, *like family*. But I couldn't tell my father not to come. I couldn't risk hurting him. *What if he waits outside the hospital?* I offered, and we went on this way, back and forth, negotiating.

In the end, we arranged that my dad would pick me up at the train, the morning of my mother's surgery, drive me to the hospital, wait around until she'd gone under, then *maybe* come inside and wait with me. It all seemed pointless to me, and I tried to passively urge him not to come. "It's really not a big deal," I repeated, but he insisted. And when I exited the station that morning, scanning the street for my father's car, I remember feeling relieved, looking forward to my father's control, comforting in a crisis.

I approached the car. Time slowed as I reached for the handle, then withdrew my hand suddenly, as if I'd been burned. The drama teacher was sitting in the passenger seat. Everything went blurry as my mind raced to reorganize itself. How could he have brought her to this? How could he not have told me? I wanted to scream. I wanted to punch him repeatedly. I wanted to cry. But instead I swallowed the lump in my throat, blinked my eyes, and climbed into the backseat, smiling and making small talk as we drove the few short blocks to the hospital, then urging them to just drop me by the entrance. *Maybe we could meet for lunch,* my father offered. *Maybe.* I nodded. I walked into the hospital alone.

■ ■ ■ ■

In pre-op, my mother's friends gathered round, kissing her cheek, assuring her they'd see her on the other side. They left one by one, exiting the curtained staging area, then waiting outside in the hospital hallway. Soon we were alone. She looked small on the gurney, shower-capped and crying. I towered over her, dry-eyed but suddenly a child, frightened and ashamed. *What's happening?* I wanted to ask her, or someone, anyone. I searched my mind for numbers to count, a structure to lean on, while I looked down at my mother's face, sticky with tears. We were silent for a long time before she told me she loved me. She knew even then what she wanted her last words to be.

"I love you, too," I said, and felt relieved and sunken afterward because it was so true. And yet she had often thought it wasn't. She had said as much — *You don't love me* — when I refused to change for her, refused therapy, and refused her attempts at intervention. "You're all spirit," she had said, "you are a girl in trouble." We waged war over the battlefield of my body, even after I left for college. Over the outside of it, how it looked, what anyone could read from my dark circles and jutting collar-bones. She was terrified for me, she told me. *What will become of you?* she asked. At the time I couldn't tell what she meant, not really. But now I think that her fear for me was inseparable from her fear for herself. What would become of me? she wanted to know, because she was terrified she wouldn't live long enough to save me herself.

She stayed under for hours, although the exact number has been lost for me among all the operations that followed, all the other hours. I waited with her friends until I could stand their company no longer, and re-treated to the cafeteria with some textbooks. But I couldn't read, couldn't focus. I just sat, staring mindlessly at the indoor foun-tain, the water cascading, recycling, and returning, the way I imagined it might come from me if I let it, an endless supply of tears. When my father called to check in, I an-swered, ready to dodge lunch. But he was at IKEA anyway, shopping with the drama teacher.

It was evening by the time my mother's surgeon came out and gave the okay. I made some excuse about class in the morning and left, climbing back into my father's car, then back onto a train to New York. I didn't want to make him wait, didn't want to tell him to go home and leave me here, either. I could see it was important to him to feel like he'd helped me with this. I didn't want to let him down, then suffer the consequences later.

Back in my dorm room, I stood in the shower and ran the water as hot as I could take it, my skin turning the raw pink of a fresh burn. I needed to feel something, anything. I was afraid I'd forgotten how. Beneath the beating water, cloaked by steam and the rattle of the fan, I sobbed dry tears. They were all I could muster.

The next day was a Wednesday, a class day, and I went about my business as if nothing had happened. I was scheduled to return to New Haven on Friday afternoon, following my last class, and I occupied those two days with everything but my mother. It was only in dreams that I encountered her. Beneath the cover of sleep it seemed my dreams melded with hers. There I saw her, shadowed by a wash of opiate-den purple and painkiller blue, helpless and alone.

She was still in ICU when I arrived on Friday, propped up and yellow in the white-sheeted bed, with Judy in the plastic armchair beside her, wiping her dry lips with a green sponge on a stick. "She's in and out," Judy told me. But I could tell my mother could feel me there, hear my voice. I could tell because she kept her eyes closed, stayed shrouded in dream, but shook her head and furrowed her brow and said *Don't let him in here, do not let him in here,* over and over, while we all pretended not to know what she was talking about.

This was the first time I'd seen my mother this way, drugged and debilitated. I remember thinking during that visit how dead she looked. But I shrugged off the shock of it, took her to the bathroom to pee, or try to. This was the first time I placed the urine hat, smelled the fluid she emitted, concentrated and soupy, her very own bone stock. She could already walk, and the nurses showed me how to hoist her from bed so that we could shuffle the halls, she holding the rolling bar of IV bags and cords, and me holding her elbow, her waist. Judy was on the phone. "Yes, she's here," I heard her say, "she's walking her mother down the hallway," and I remember feeling relieved that for once I hadn't disappointed. For once my obsession with perfection hadn't kept me from my mother's side.

23

I'd relied on sugar-free Jell-O as a safe food throughout high school, but during my first year of college, sugar-free Jell-O *pudding* also became a staple of my diet. I liked the little cups it came in in the cafeteria, and bought extra from the Gristedes down the street to keep in my mini fridge. It was smooth and sweet and sixty calories per cup. If placed in the freezer for a half hour, it became akin to soft-serve ice cream. Each bite was an allowed indulgence, exactly what the Kraft Foods marketing department wanted it to be. I ate it guiltlessly and with relief.

Jell-O's appearance in my college cafeteria, and in others around the country, is part and parcel of a wider food-service presence Kraft cultivated over the years. For decades, Jell-O has been served in schools, jails, and hospitals. Everyone eats Jell-O, particularly when sick, not only because it molds itself nicely to restricted diets, but because it melts in the mouth from a relative solid to liquid, making it an easy segue into solid food for patients recently out of surgery — patients like my mother. Although at first she rarely partook, she was given Jell-O after each surgery. It arrived on her tray like a consolation, a lighthearted food to distract from the pain of resection. She saw it as irony, an emblem of what had made her ill in the first place. Even so, she received it with humor. When I was little, she passed it off to me. When I was older she offered it to her roommate. At the end of her life she allowed it, her acceptance a sign of resignation, a sign of the end, a sign I didn't know to look for.

Jell-O's established place in hospitals, and as a sick food in general, has recently waned. It may melt in the mouth, and Jell-O *may* be comfortingly nostalgic, but it's also laden with concerning chemicals, so much so that in Europe (where Jell-O is less popular) boxes come marked with a warning label referencing the product's use of artificial dyes and ingredients. Specifically, Jell-O contains red dye number 40 and BHA, both linked to health risks, as well as an array of unnamed "artificial flavors," most likely petroleum derived, and gelatin obtained from factory-farm leftovers.

Nary a hospital nutritionist, nary even an eating disorder nutritionist, I would come to find out, has called out Jell-O's health concerns. But the recent cultural push for whole, antibiotic-free, natural food has resulted in some hospitals' changing their menus anyway, swapping out white bread and pasta for whole wheat, for example, or offering cage-free eggs and unmedicated meat. Jell-O remains widely circulated in institutional settings, but, given this shift, it's only a matter of time before it gets nixed altogether.

"I don't see how forcing us to eat a thousand calories of this crap is going to help anything," Grace said. She was seated in one of the big armchairs, legs pulled up to her chest, elbows on her knees. "Like," she went on, "the other night my boyfriend and I were walking and we stopped at Burger King and he was trying to get me to eat and I was like, *I legitimately don't want that.* I know I'm *disordered* or whatever, but I'm also fucking sick of poisoning my body." Around the room other girls nodded. Some just stared blankly or looked down at the pillows they hugged tight, like children, in their laps. I scanned the room before fixing my gaze back on Grace's face. Her skin was clear, makeup-free. She looked effortlessly clean. I craved that cleanness, a naturalness I wondered if I could ever achieve. It was a feeling akin to the desire for safety, the pleasurable emptiness, that had fed my compulsions. Now, though, it was a desire I wanted to fulfill healthily. I wanted to safeguard my body with health foods. Whole heads of fresh green broccoli. Thick strips of meaty salmon. I wanted it all to nourish me. I wanted it all to pin me to the earth.

But even here, at a center in midtown Manhattan dedicated to treating adolescent eating disorders and their attendant mental health issues, the artificial safe foods I'd eaten for years were easy to find. Even Jell-O — albeit in its full-sugar form — was on the menu. At the communal meals we patients shared and processed, Jell-O pudding was a dessert option at least twice a week. I ordered it when I could, which wasn't often. Diversity was what we were supposed to strive for by taking on "trigger foods" in the center's safe environment. Typical safe foods like steamed vegetables and fruit were mostly disallowed.

One night, I challenged myself to try the pizza, which reminded me of happy times with my dad. I peeled open the Styrofoam container it came in and transferred the food onto a paper plate. The slice looked like it had been microwaved; the cheese, now turning cold and hard, had been frozen before. I lifted it to my mouth and bit. The room stayed upright, the world spun on. Afterward, when we went around the table, each of us sharing what our meals had raised for us, I said the pizza had turned out to be just pizza. I'd feared that eating it would uncover a sinkhole of sadness and anger, threatening to suck me in. But I was safe here at the center, tethered. I learned I could probe the edges of the sinkhole and know it wouldn't engulf me. A year had passed since Mary's surgery, and, though her oncologist insisted on CT scans every six months, her body was cancer-free. But healing this way had only turned my mother's focus more fully toward me. She became insistent on my treatment, finally holding tight and refusing to let go, the way I hadn't let myself ask her to.

"This isn't your fault," she told me, "but you do need help to fix it." Hearing this was the permission I needed to save myself. So when summer arrived and school let out, I voluntarily admitted myself to the center. And although I wept with nerves before the first meeting, I quickly felt encircled by a coven of women who shared my story. "How did I get here?" I asked at the first dinner, looking around the table for signs of recognition in the other girls' faces. I found them. After that I spoke often, voicing the secret compulsions that had structured my world, emboldened by the other girls' stories, uncannily similar to mine.

For three months I attended the center every other night, peeing into a cup, standing in line to be weighed, sitting at a long table with twenty other girls for our diverse communal dinners, ordered from Gigi Café, a New York panini chain known for convenience, not quality. As Grace pointed out, the system was flawed, attempting to strengthen girls' starving bodies with food that sat like canola-oil anvils in our empty stomachs. For many patients, the food was too much; the pendulum swing from denial of any food to consumption of heavy, fattening processed food was too drastic. For others it was a jump start on the binge-and-purge cycle they'd fall into once they left the center for the night and went home. For me it was a start in a good direction. Although I understood Grace's rebellion, I wanted to move toward discharge, and I knew protesting the shitty panini chain would only keep me admitted longer. Learning to truly nourish my body would be a lifelong process, the therapists kept saying, and I knew that for me, the process had to entail natural foods, homeopathic remedies, and organic ingredients, foods in line with the tradition of witchcraft — women's bodies — from which I'd been separated by my disorders. I imagined healing soups, rich with medicinal herbs, working their way through my gnarled insides, fixing me from the inside out; and cleansing juices and tonics: spirulina for my blotchy eyesight, flaxseed and golden turmeric milk to clear my skin, thicken my hair, evening primrose oil to bring back my period. I knew this approach would be ideal for me — for all of us girls at the center — and I knew it was just too expensive. So we ordered Jell-O and pizza and chicken sandwiches. We cleaned our plates, then discussed how to parse our food from our feelings. Whereas today a steady diet of Gigi Café would make me feel oily and lethargic, I was so starved when I entered the center that it brought my brain back to life. After a week I could read again. I could hold a conversation. Which isn't to say my compulsions didn't remain, or don't linger still, only that they lessened when I began to speak as much as I counted.

On art therapy nights we girls gathered around a big table covered in brown packing paper. Some girls rolled clay or cut out images from magazines for collagist explanations of their negative body image. I painted, holding the brush at its end like my mother, letting the water move color across the page. I painted women's bodies, copying Mary's images of mother-witches, powerful protectors. I painted the salt marsh outside my childhood bedroom, remembering the smell of sulfur when the tide rose up and flooded the front yard. I put my parents and myself in one corner, embracing while a dark-blue hole seeped slow and syrupy from the edge of the page into the center, threatening the whole of the canvas, threatening to consume us.

When at the end of the night we girls spoke about our art, we spoke in circles. We often talked this way about our bodies, perambulating some essential desire to erase them, as if, disembodied, we'd be free. Although we sometimes struggled to articulate it, we all knew we'd been saddled with an unbearable weight, one assigned to us at birth by a culture bent on silencing us.

Taken this way, our response was a reasonable, albeit impossible, one. Lose the body, gain the freedom. We weren't self-indulgent, hysterical, or vain, as is often theorized: we were physically protesting a cultural system bent on oppressing us. We weren't complying with it; we were trying to transcend it. The task was learning how to do so while nurturing, rather than diminishing, ourselves.

Finding a way to speak, connect, and stay embodied wasn't easy. At the center someone was constantly relapsing and regressing and disappearing from group, leaving community circles to sneak pills in the bathroom, or to wedge over the toilet and dispense with dinner, or to check into the center's inpatient locations in rural, isolated places. This was not how I wanted to spend my time. I told my mother this in an email, to which she responded in one word, "Good." We'd agreed not to speak for the first month of my treatment. If I decided my disorder was tied to her, my mother reasoned, I'd need space to plan my disentanglement. This was a journey I had to begin on my own, she said, although she would be watching from a distance, ready to join me if I asked her to.

Still, as my first month at the center faded into my second, I began to call her. When we spoke, my voice wavered, as if getting used to its own volume. We talked about my father and me, and, slowly, we talked about each other, about seeing each other. "I'm coming into the city this week," she said, and I told her, "I'll meet you." It was bright out, and hot, the day we met. I walked west to Chelsea and straight into the sun. She came out of the gallery as I was going in and our bodies touched and she wrapped her arms around me like it was instinct and my body sobbed into her shoulder, all instinct. "You came back," she said. It was a return; it was an answer.

24

In 1883, French physician Auguste Fabre wrote that "all women are hysterical . . . and what constitutes the temperament of a woman is rudimentary hysteria." Hence the imperative to rein women in, confine them like animals to suburban landscapes, ranch-style homes, kitchens ornamented in charming copper molds. Hence the imperative to mistrust my mother, and scores of women before her, when they arrived in the exam room, dressed in their paper gowns, sure that something was wrong. Hence the tendency to see the anorexic, bulimic, obsessive-compulsive woman as *disordered* and *vain* rather than the logical product of the culture she's grown up in. But it's always easier, doctors quickly learn, to pat your patient on the knee, tell her she's crazy, abnormal, bad, give her some Valium, and send her home. It's always easier when she's been primed her whole life to believe you.

The term *hysteria* derives from the Greek word for "womb" and is a diagnosis at least as ancient as the case documented on a scroll of Egyptian papyrus in 1990 B.C. describing an affliction of the uterus, which caused irregular movements of the mind and body. Hippocrates traced hysterics to "wandering" wombs, nonconformist wombs, wombs that refused their prescribed role, refused wifedom, motherhood, a life dedicated to the perfection of modern housekeeping and Jell-O salads.

Diagnoses of hysteria in the Christian era linked the condition to witchcraft and satanic passion, so the association between hysteria and femininity naturally persisted, perpetuated by the witch archetype and by medical science, whose stance generally concurred with Fabre's. Not surprisingly, in the Hellenistic and medieval eras, anorexia was also often linked to witchcraft, with documented cases suggesting that the onset of the disease stemmed from ritualistic fasting the patient started, but, like a miscast spell, couldn't stop. In the nineteenth century, medical science shifted to considering anorexia nervosa less as witchcraft than hysteria (although the two are covertly linked), but it was not formally named until Sir William Gull, personal physician to Queen Victoria, published his seminal study *Anorexia Nervosa (Apepsia Hysterica, Anorexia Hysterica)* in 1873.

With the rise of the psychoanalytic doctrine of Sigmund Freud, the term *conversion* was added to *hysteria* to connote the patient's conversion of sexual impulse and emotional trauma into physical symptoms. This repressed impulse or trauma might also, according to Freud, convert itself into anorexic behavior. In his 1896 essay "The Aetiology of Hysteria," Freud suggests that hysteria *may* be decoupled from female physiology (although later in the essay he qualifies this claim) and linked instead to one's upbringing, making men susceptible to hysteria and broaching the concept that hysteria could be a social disease — although, as I learned in Women's Studies 101, in Freud's practical work, the patient was almost always female.

Then came feminism to suggest that isolating women from nature and each other, confining us to the kitchen, convincing us we were competitors rather than allies, calling us crazy if we strayed from prescribed roles, had been a ploy of the patriarchy all along. Dora was right to abandon her treatment, many feminist scholars proclaimed; she was right to claim Freud didn't understand her because she was a woman. Besides, women weren't more vain, jealous, dependent, or submissive than men, as was argued in Freud's famous (and somewhat disastrous) lecture on femininity. Nor were they less moral or less loving. Nor did they harbor a collective and poisonous penis envy.

These complaints fed a movement pointed at *reclaiming* hysteria, a movement best summed up by theorist Elaine Showalter, who writes of hysteria "as a specifically feminine protolanguage, communicating via the body messages that cannot be verbalized." But though Showalter's attempt to take ownership of this protolanguage was mirrored by many other academics, outside the ivory tower the trope of the madwoman, the hysteric, persists. In fact, we've dedicated a whole genre of reality television to the schadenfreude of watching her enact her hysteria. In this genre, "real housewives" of various cities wage brutal war against each other, often devolving into shouting matches and physical violence. These women have become celebrities. But they are also cultural laughingstocks, dismissed for their unstable behavior on screen and their obvious addictions to plastic surgery. But what if, like the anorexic, these women are searching for freedom from their bodies? If they can achieve the impossible, if they can cheat time, cheat genetics, they'll be free.

Even if the real housewives are more radical, more empathic, than they seem, the cultural response to their "hysterics" was just the response the girls of LeRoy would refuse in 2011, when they insisted their illness had a *real* source, a physical source. Of course, my mother and I both agreed, the reason for the girls' illness could be anything. But physical or not, it would always be *real.* "This is exactly what happened to me when you were a little girl," Mary said, remembering how she fought for the surgery that saved her life. "No wonder they want there to be a physical reason for their symptoms; it's the only way anyone will take them seriously."

My mother was frustrated that twenty years after her first diagnosis, people were still telling women that their suffering was imagined. But I was frustrated by the girls' inability to accept their own trauma. "I really don't think that any of us had that traumatic of a life before," Katie Krautwurst insisted. But Katie's mom, Beth, a patient with a facial nerve condition called trigeminal neuralgia, was often in agonizing pain. By the time Katie awoke from her nap in 2011 with her own face in spasm, her mother had undergone a total of thirteen brain surgeries. At the time I wondered how Katie couldn't see in her body what I did as it ticked and twitched — the depth of her pain; her mother's illness, the fear and helplessness it had imprinted upon her and the legacy of loss she'd inherited simply by being born a woman.

Now, though, I think her radical. Her mother, too. I think all the girls of LeRoy, in insisting they be heard, in insisting they not be passed off as crazy, were radical, even as I think them subject to that unspoken legacy. *I know my daughter,* the mothers insisted. *She's happy.* Not damaged, not bad, not malingering or rotten on the inside, like today's real housewives, or the instigator of the Salem trials, at least in Arthur Miller's version. In *The Crucible,* one of literature's most popular explorations of female hysteria — and one cited an awful lot in relationship to the LeRoy girls — conversion disorder is presented as a revelation of women's *true nature* when left in the pressure cooker of oppressive culture for too long. The girls in Salem easily turn feral in Miller's play, accusing each other wildly to save themselves. And at the root of it all? A man. Abigail Williams, obsessed with the already-married John Proctor, incites mass hysteria and hangs half the town, all in an effort to take him for herself. The other girls follow along like lambs. So no wonder the girls of LeRoy resisted their diagnosis: to accept it would only take their story from them, cast them in the same mold as the Salem girls, brainless and boy crazy, in need of masculine rationalism to diagnose and cure them. Rather, they wanted to be seen for what they were; they wanted to be believed on their own terms.

25

Autumn. Leaves falling, rattling as they blew. This was my first Thanksgiving in years spent with my mother, and we were joined by Judy and a slew of other family friends. I'd spent the last holiday alone in my dorm room, eating ramen noodles, the nutritional content of which I knew exactly. What did I give thanks to then? Freedom to stand at the microwave and count, to know exactly how many calories I consumed. Just a year before, that had seemed more important than being around people or feeling wanted and loved. I was self-conscious about my problem, which was obvious, visible in my bony body, which ticked and twitched at the height of my illness, the height of my silence, with everything I wanted to confess but couldn't yet articulate.

So here I was, a year later, in recovery, wearing the winter jacket Mary had bought me, stepping off the train in Connecticut and wheeling my suitcase toward the beams of her headlights. "Don't you look pretty," she said when I got in. We leaned across the gear stick to kiss each other's cheeks.

"Let's park for a minute," she said.

"What's wrong?" I asked, already bracing myself against the familiar sense of disappointment and loss rising up inside me.

"Well, it's about the CT scan I had the other day?"

I nodded, already knowing.

"The tumors," she said, "they're back."

For a moment I didn't speak, just searched her face for how she might be feeling. "How can this be happening?" I finally managed. It had been only a year and a half since her surgery.

"I don't know," she said, and we were quiet again, stretched across the console of her car to hug, unable to get close enough. "But I just got you back," I said, starting to cry.

"We'll figure something out," she said into my shoulder, "we'll fix it."

I didn't ask how. Just lingered close to her warm body, unwilling to let go first. But there were people waiting at the house, and she broke away.

■ ■ ■ ■

A week later, we went to the specialist together, carrying binders of bloodwork and medical records. The office was on the Upper East Side, the surgeon inside it white-haired and small. Mary had fought for a referral to see him, and he sat across a cluttered mahogany desk from us, shuffling paperwork and sighing as if our presence exhausted him. When he unearthed her charts, he examined them, saying nothing, and I thought nothing, not knowing to be afraid; my mother's voice had been so sure that night at the train station. *We'll fix it,* she had said.

"These aren't operable," the surgeon finally said. "It's too risky."

Mary leaned forward. "There's nothing we can do?"

He shrugged. "I've seen worse," he said. "I've seen tumors like this go on without growth for years." We must have looked hopeful, because he held out his hand. "Judging by this chart, though," he said, "I'd give you three years."

"Three years until what?" I asked, looking at my mother, who was looking at him. Nobody answered.

We left the office in a blur, and she began to walk downtown, but I caught her arm and said, "Hold on a minute. Let's just take a breath here." We faced each other. We hugged. "Fuck him," she said.

With surgery off the table, Mary chose a course of chemotherapy suspected, but not proven, to shrink neuroendocrine tumors like hers. I would spend winter break in Connecticut, we decided. I would give her the daily shot.

On a Friday afternoon, sitting in an empty chemotherapy infusion room just before the office closed, we were shown how the shot was administered. The sky outside was already dark blue, the color of despair. But we were optimistic. It was the only bearable response.

A blond nurse rushed in with a pillow and a syringe. "Look," she said, demonstrating with quick efficiency how to pull from the vial and clear air bubbles, before poking the needle unceremoniously into the pillow's bulk. When she leaned in to trace exactly where on my mother's thigh I'd inject the drugs, I could see the spots where lipstick had stuck to her dry, flaking lips. Maybe I was imagining it, but up close the nurse seemed warmer, maternal but firm, toward both Mary and me. She could see we were both childlike around the needle. She guided our hands over the pillow prop with careful patience, demonstrating how to hold the syringe, how to shoot the trigger. "Not so bad," I said when we were done, emboldened by the nurse's lesson. I looked at my mother, who looked back, worried. Eventually I'd have to return to school, and she'd have to give the shot to herself. The importance of this self-reliance was stressed by our teacher-nurse. "It's really not hard," she said, and we agreed obediently, unwilling to say what we both were thinking: the shot was poison, but it was poison my mother needed to live. At home Mary wrestled with her fear of the venomous chemicals, sitting on the edge of her bed and holding the syringe over her leg. Her breath would shorten. "I just can't do it," she'd gasp, fear fuzzing the edges of her voice.

Eventually she opted for a less invasive regime, given weekly at her oncologist's office. "It's just not worth the torture," she said.

Friday afternoons I came in from the city to sit with her in side-by-side chemo-ward armchairs, surrounded by gray bodies hooked to infusions, and the nurses who circulated with snack bags and juice boxes, little plastic cups of red Jell-O. Then we'd go into a small room, and she'd bend over an exam table with her pants around her ankles, holding my hand and making bad jokes while a nurse pushed a long needle into the bruised skin of her ass. Each time I watched this process, I felt the contorted pain on my mother's face in my own body. It lodged beneath my breastbone, a dull breathlessness. But the sensation passed quickly. She was always resilient. She'd stand, give herself a little shake, and smile. "Glad that's over," she'd say.

Months and then a year passed quickly. My mother traveled — trips to Guatemala, Morocco, and Spain, where she sat with her sketchbook, always surrounded by crowds of children, angling to get a look. I graduated, got a job. Mary gave me a puppy, and he grew. The tumors did not. "I made a deal with them," she said. "What was your deal?" I asked. She ignored the question, and I didn't push. I wanted to believe it was possible to barter for her survival.

When she began to limp, wincing with each step, her pain took up residence in my body, too. For her it was raw nerve, slipped disks, not cancer but the sensation of constant sciatica. For me it was the pain of preemptive grief, a pain I'd live with for years to come. But, we were assured by a new team of doctors, the back was fixable. "We'll cut here," the lead surgeon said, holding his pen like a pointer to show us how he'd make two incisions, peel the skin back and fuse what he found broken. Mary nodded. She was eager for mobility, and freedom. "I have places to go," she said, and I thought of her, four years before, lying like a husk of herself in the hospital bed, hopped up on painkillers and telling me she wanted me to know that she'd never do that again. *I just want you to know this,* she had said. *It's important you know this.* She was crying, and the artificial lights above her bed made the tears crease her face like laugh lines.

Now she was adamant. The pain was too great, the back must be mended. So she scheduled the operation for January, and I quit my job and moved into her attic to serve as caretaker during the months of recovery the surgery required. "Are you sure about this?" she kept asking. I was sure. Something had shifted. I wanted to stabilize, to release the compulsions that had kept me from her side. My mother had protected me by urging me into recovery. Now I wanted to protect her.

It snowed. The surgeon cut. Mary's friend, my beloved "unkie" Richard, arrived, and we sat together in the waiting room, which emptied as the hours passed, first six, then eight, then twelve. It was after midnight when we were allowed to see her, covered in Betadine stains and pallid yellow bruises. "She looks like she's had the shit beat out of her," Richard said, and I thought about seeing her after the liver resection three years before, how she looked like she'd been skinned, segmented, and pieced back together. Now, having been cut to the bone, she looked worse than before.

She woke the next morning angry and confused, then drifted away again. She clicked the Call button by her side to summon nurses she then eyed with suspicion. "They're poisoning me," she said conspiratorially, as if she knew she could trust me to understand her paranoia, her fear of being silenced. But I wasn't yet ready to bear her helplessness. I wasn't yet ready to assume the mother role. I guessed it was the drugs, removing my mother from herself, ferrying her into darkness. But what if it wasn't? I needed her to tell me, and because she couldn't, I brushed her off, packed up my things, and left for the night.

Later, after I'd gone to her house and walked her dogs, made myself soup and gone to bed, she called. I felt the phone buzzing from underneath my pillow where I'd tucked it, close enough to wake me should an emergency arise. "Mom," I said, sitting up in bed, "what's wrong?"

"It's in my IV," she said unceremoniously.

"What is?" I asked her.

"Strychnine," she whispered matter-of-factly. I felt myself spring from the residue of a dream, as she had each time I went to her as a child, frightened by a nightmare and unable to return to sleep. I pictured Midge in her housecoat, reaching for her daughter, my mother, begging *Hide me* as the ambulance approached. I wanted to take my mother seriously, to hear her fears, her voice. So I called the nurse's station on her floor and explained that my mother wasn't feeling well. "She's expressed concerns," I told the first nurse I spoke to, whose voice was thick with sleep and annoyance. She'd look into it, she said. I hit Redial repeatedly, talked to whoever I could. I knew I was getting a reputation on the floor, one to match my mother's. I wanted to tell each person I spoke to, each pink-scrubbed nurse at the desk, the story of the last time my mother saw her mother. I wanted to tell them that it played in my head, an endless reel of regret that colored Mary's life. *This is why,* I wanted to say. *This explains it all.* But instead I compulsively apologized, said *sorry* like a tic, verbal evidence of my girlhood.

It was cold and quiet and lonely on her floor, which seemed, unlike the cancer ward we'd grown used to, abandoned. Days passed, and then a week. She woke from her opiate dream from time to time, long enough to pick out the cute nurse and call me to report his shift times. "McDreamy is on tonight," she'd say, and I'd smile in the mirror before I left the house because she was getting better.

We giggled each time McDreamy rushed past her room, a blur in his blue scrubs. When he came inside to do vitals or check Mary's IV, she batted her eyelashes, and I asked questions about what the ticking orange numbers illuminated on the screen above her bed meant, what they promised. She was often happy when I left, clear-headed and content, but would call me later, after I'd gone home and she'd fallen asleep and awoken again. I'd look at the clock. Listen to her complain. "Let's face it," she said once, "I'm all alone." I could hear the morphine in her voice.

"Not true," I said. "Don't say that."

She sounded angry. "But I am," she insisted. "I am I am I am entirely alone."

After a week, the medevac arrived to take her to rehab. She gripped my arms tightly as I pulled her to an upright seat. Together we swung one of her legs, then the other, out from under the covers of her bed. She stood, holding my hands, looking out the door and down the hallway. "I think I can do it," she said to the attendant, waiting in the doorframe with a wheelchair, but he apologized, told her he had to push her, and she sank into the seat.

I followed the van to Madison House, a one-story building in the shape of a horse-shoe. It blended in with January, a bleak, unfinished circle. Inside, wheelchairs lined the hallways. It smelled of unemptied bed-pans and microwaved mashed potatoes. Most of the patients, we discovered, were permanent guests over the age of eighty. "We can leave," I told my mother, knowing that she couldn't.

Her room was at the very end of a long pink hallway hung with silk screens of sailboats and teddy bears. Her roommate, Meg, had just had her uterus removed. "Happy to have someone to talk to," she said. But my mother wanted nothing to do with her. Each day when I visited, she'd turn in bed to face me, wincing as she went, then roll her eyes, stick out her tongue, and point her thumb backward, through her torso, at Meg. "She is very fat," my mother would whisper when Meg was in the bathroom. "Mom," I'd say. I was often angry with her, exasperated and embarrassed by the drugs' coloring everything she said, their effects blanketing her mind in mean hopelessness. "Everything hurts," she repeatedly said. "Everything is a mess." The bathroom was flecked with the drops of dried blood Meg leaked with each step she took. She often left the urine hat on the toilet. "It's disgusting in here," my mother said, holding up her hands as if anything she touched would contaminate her. She told the nurses, loudly, how *disgusting* it was. Meg never seemed to notice. She talked about the weather, her favorite TV shows. She gave too much advice. "Can't she see I don't care?" my mother said. "No," I said, "but I can. You don't seem to care about anything."

She was getting worse. She wouldn't eat, and the nurses were exasperated. They removed her untouched trays, the tinfoil-topped containers of Jell-O I jokingly bribed her with. She craved only wonton soup, she told me, so I drove to First Garden every day and returned with a hot container of broth and dumplings. I carried the soup from the car, wrapped in my jacket, holding it bundled like a baby through the stinking hallway to her room, where she was staring at the clock, into it, past it.

She was calm the night before she left. Meg was already gone, readmitted to Yale because she couldn't stop bleeding. She was frightened when she left, and my mother was tender and concerned, an improvement, I thought. "Not you," I told her after we'd watched Meg's gurney disappear through the door. "You're going home." She closed her eyes and smiled, squeezed my hand. "One o'clock is the earliest we can discharge her," the nurse said when she stopped by the room to remove Meg's sheets. "See you at one," I said to my mother when I left, kissing her cheek.

When I arrived the next day at 1:15, she was sitting on her bed with her head in her hands. "Hi," I said, and she looked up, tearstained. "Where were you?" she said. Her words were accusatory, desperate. "I

285

thought —" she said, "I thought something happened to you. I imagined the worst." She began to cry in earnest, and I went to her side. "Get me out of here," she said, rocking back and forth, her face in her palms, "please please get me out of here."

In my memory I run behind her wheel-chair, push her out of Madison House and over to the car feverishly, like I am stealing her away. I throw her into the backseat and peel off, home free. I know, however, that I walked her slowly, even as she told me to hurry. We passed the parked wheelchairs, the doors flung open to dusky blue rooms and flashing TV screens. I told her *Get ready* when the automatic doors drew apart to let us pass and the January cold washed over us.

I picture myself that day, so measured and calm, and wonder what I could have done better. What would have happened if I'd truly run behind my mother's wheelchair? Broken all the rules, screamed *fuck you* like a wild woman to the herd of white-coated doctors lurking in the hallways? Would doing so have given me the power to be a better caretaker than I was? I wanted to be my mother's protector, a sorceress capable of healing her wounds. And maybe I was. But most of my memories of my mother's illnesses are of my own childishness, the numb annoyance that covered over my fear.

By March, Mary was walking again, eating normally, looking forward to getting back into her studio, getting back to her memoir. When the time came for a routine CT scan, she followed the familiar drill, drinking the contrast, lying perfectly still while her body was fed through the doughnut-shaped machine, and following up the next week with her oncologist, Dr. Saif.

It had been three years since we'd sat in that surgeon's office while he shook his head, saying there was nothing to be done. And in that time Mary's tumors had stayed small and steady, held there by shots, or spells, or both. So we'd become accustomed to our visits to Dr. Saif as lengthy routines always resulting in remarks on how miraculous it was that the tumors hadn't grown. "Just stay the course," we'd grown used to hearing, as a team of harried interns waved us out the door.

These clipboard-laden interns were everywhere at Saif's, always preceding his coming, striding into the room where we waited to report to us Mary's entire medical history, as if they were informing us of what we did not already know. This time, however, the latest scholar read too much off his clipboard and revealed the bad news Dr. Saif was slated to break, then left the room while we sat in shocked silence, absorbing *substantial growth.* "Maybe he made a mistake," I kept saying while my mother silently shifted in her chair, hands on her knees, waiting for Saif, who took another thirty minutes to arrive and confirm what his student had let slip.

The tumors were suddenly big enough to cut out, at least partly, and surgery was scheduled in an emergency capacity. Judy arrived to serve as co-caretaker. Richard came, too. We three sat together in the waiting room, measuring hours in cups of tea, trips to the bathroom, pages of the *New York Times.* A day passed. Judy and Richard went home to feed the dogs, and I waited alone, the only person left in the communal waiting area, for the verdict. "I scraped tumors off the abdominal scar from 1992," Mary's latest surgeon, Dr. Cha, said when finally he appeared. "I ablated three from the liver, resected a good portion, and got another two." "Swiss cheesed her," I said, and he looked confused. He told me there were also tumors nestled in her bowels. "I resected what I could of all that, too," he said. When I thanked him, he told me it was my responsibility to know that they would come back. He'd debulked her, he said, so it could be many years from now — she could outlive them. But it was my responsibility to know.

The anesthesia wore off rapidly. They released her early. The strength she mustered to get herself home quickly waned. She began hallucinating and vomiting. She would not eat. The leaves on the trees outside her window unfurled in spurts of white-tipped green, the way they always do in Connecticut in the early summer. But the color inside was dark, indistinct. There were caterpillars in the drapery, she told me, monsters on the wall.

When she finally asked for food, it was as a starving person asks, desperately. I packed up my purse and walked the aisles of the colossal suburban grocery store, feeling small among the towering shelves of brightly colored boxes. I filled the cart with all her favorite sick foods: canned soup and ramen noodles, chocolate-covered raisins, boxes of pasta and saltine crackers, hunks of French bread, ginger ale. But she ate none of it, save for small portions of Lay's potato chips from a bright-yellow bag she carried around the house with her as she began to walk again, her coming always marked by the shuffle of her slippers, the crinkle of the bag.

As she ate, her body shrank, regressing into something primordial. She grew scales. Layers of flaky dead cells that no amount of scrubbing and exfoliating could slough off. I took to sitting by her bed each night before she slept and working on her feet, translucent and bloodless, her legs, cold and peppered with tufts of unshaven hair. Touching her worried me. It was as if I were touching a drowned person's body — dewy but cold and fish-bone white. Still I came, bearing pumice stone and lotions I laid out performatively, and filing away dead skin in unending layers, dustings of her on the bedsheets, the floor, to be swept away until tomorrow.

When Dr. Cha closed the surgery, he glued Mary back together. He did not bolt back into one the two sides of her stomach with three-inch surgical staples that leave scars like vampire bites, as the surgeons did after her second resection. Instead he slathered surgical glue over the edges of her open body and folded one side of her skin over the other.

"This will make for prettier scar," he'd told me in the consultation room.

"What happened to her old scars?" I'd asked.

There were little tumors affixed to the old tissue like barnacles. "I cut them out," he'd said.

Each day when I lifted my mother's nightgown to clean the incision, there was only a clean strip of skin with a thin line zigzagging gracefully through the space between her sternum and her hips, like the hairline cracks over the face of an egg before the shell shatters and the yolk slips out.

This was 2009, two years before the outbreak in LeRoy. But the seeds of the girls' illness were already taking root. This is something the media rarely covered in 2011, when the outbreak emerged in earnest. The girls in LeRoy had all been party to traumatic events several years prior to the onset of their symptoms. Two years before the outbreak in LeRoy, Thera Sanchez suffered a traumatic loss her family chose not to publicize. She began to twitch. But at the time, her symptoms were self-contained and subsided on their own, and nobody thought much of them. In February of 2009, Lydia Parker — another girl who in 2011 would alternate between paralysis and twitching, voicelessness and stuttering — reported that she threw a shoe at her father when he came home drunk. He then hit her in the head and backed her into a corner, where the two punched each other repeatedly. Meanwhile, Katie Krautwurst, the first LeRoy girl to develop symptoms, watched her mother suffer through thirteen surgeries.

But normalization is a peculiar human strength. After each trauma they experienced, the girls' lives likely rebalanced themselves, seeking equilibrium by instinct. I picture them returning with relief to the routines of school and cheerleading, the inconsequential dramas circulating through their friend group. Maybe Katie and Lydia and Thera were emboldened, at least at first, by their hardships. Maybe they felt stronger for them, like they knew now how to handle every challenge life delivered; knew to numb out, talk on the phone, go to bed and wake to morning rituals. Maybe, like me, they leaned on those rituals. Maybe, like me, they even constructed new ones to control a world they already understood could change suddenly and without warning, trauma returning like prophecy, or curse.

June rain. I stood by the window outside the downstairs bathroom door, watching it fall, waiting to help my mother back to bed. The door opened slowly, and she came out, looking confused, her hands clasped over a patch of nightgown that was blood spattered — rusty red and orange over blue patterned flowers. "We may need to call for help," she said, removing her hands as if revealing a mistake. "Let me see," I said from my closed throat, lifting her gown to look at the incision, finding it split, red blossoms leaking out.

In the emergency room, Dr. Cha bent over my mother, wearing his dinner jacket, casually cutting through surgical glue and sinew and skin. I sat in a plastic chair outside and peeked around the drape, watching him move with studied indifference from scalpel to suction. Watching blood, flowing fast through thin tube, be vacuumed away, then swabbed with sterile gauze the way warm bread sops up last spoonfuls of soup.

He wanted to admit her, he said, so he could pump her with antibiotics and prevent another hematoma. A nurse named Chaps, with bleached-blond hair and a spray tan, gave me graham crackers and a juice box before untethering my mother from her wires and wheeling her bed out of triage and into a narrow hallway. "We'll stick you here for now," she said. Then she was gone.

As the night wore on, I lost time to hopeful

waiting, a state of expectation in which hours sped past. My mother and I picked out a new McDreamy, and I occupied myself with trying to get his attention. When he brought me an unsolicited blanket, a juice box, a carton of Jell-O, his offerings felt like triumphs. Mary watched as I spooned the wiggling pink into my mouth. "I'm so hungry," she said.

"This is gross," I said, guiltily putting the carton down. Food was forbidden for her, a contaminant.

"No, no, don't stop," she said, always finding comfort in the sight of me eating.

"It's okay," I said. "Be right back." I tossed the empty cup into the trash and walked around the corner, pretending I needed to pee but looking for more Jell-O, which I found and ate, two more cartons' worth, to cover the hunger I imagined my mother felt.

Days later we went home with more stitches, but they would split twice more before Cha would say he'd had enough and settle on leaving a gaping wound, a watermelon-sized hole in Mary's torso that had to heal from the inside out without contamination or infection.

"Anything else will just make more fistulas and hematomas," he told me, manhandling the wound, poking and prodding it like something alive, a deep-sea creature. It smelled fetid and human and filled the whole room. My mother held her hands up and closed her eyes, as she would come to do whenever it was spread open before her. She didn't want to see herself, and no one thought she should. This wound was the stuff of nightmares, and hers remained painkiller thick. At night she called for help, yelling, *Judy! Allie!* from her hospital bed in the sunroom, the same one we'd rented for the back surgery five months before. I'd hear her, then listen for Judy getting out of bed one floor below. If she went, I figured, I could remain frozen beneath the covers, staring at the ceiling, frightened of my own mother, who had become both childlike and monstrous in her illness. She gaped at me, a bottomless pit of need in a broken woman's body. I did what I could to save and protect her.

I did what I could, but it felt impossible. I felt impossibly inadequate. I knew the price of hiding beneath the sheets, behind the shed; I knew the price of running. All my life I'd heard the story of the last time Mary saw Midge, the guilt she'd quietly carried and how it'd turned to sickness inside her. I wanted to avoid her fate, but there were moments during her care that I froze, unable to speak or move, unable to treat her with the kindness I wished I could muster. My mother was *my* protector. Now, faced with being hers, I felt small, unprepared, and, at times, irrationally angry with her for putting me in this position. I wanted her to reach for me, to hold me tight, to tell me she would be okay. But, lost in her pain and the hazy place she went to escape it, all she could do was frown, meet my eyes, and mouth *ouch,* both of us knowing there was nothing I could do to help.

On good days I tried, arriving at her bedside for pedicures or back rubs, walking her to the shower, where she sat in a plastic chair, holding her stomach and offering up one leg and then the other for me to shave. On good days I performed these functions as I would for myself. Her body was my body — the two of us were connected by an energetic umbilical cord always jerking me back to her even as I wanted to run, too afraid to face her gruesome form. Her body foretold a lonely future, but it was the only one I had.

26

The history of witchcraft, like the history of the domestic-science movement and the Jell-O it loved, is a history of women's work and women's relationships. It is a history of caretaking and healing passed from woman to woman. How to birth a child, how to keep a pregnancy, how to end one, how to heal a wound. It is a history of a sphere outside patriarchy that has fought for centuries to survive, depending on oral traditions, the imprint of past experiences on the XX chromosome, the knowledge that goes with it. It is the history of religion and capitalism, politics, violence, feminized poverty; the separation of women from their bodies and each other, and the persecution of those who attempt to reconnect.

It is the history of feminism, of Cixous and Clément's "Sorceress and Hysteric," a section of their seminal *Newly Born Woman*. In it they explore Freud's famous hysterical subject Emmy von N., suggesting that she showed an inherent understanding, internalization, and performance of the female suffering that preceded her. Through hysteria, Emmy von N. "was able to repeat in the register of symptoms all the history written in feminine mythologies." In other words, "the hysteric resumes and assumes the memories of others." Put another way: *the repressed survives in woman.*

This concept of women as conduits — dare I say vessels — for the past is what my mother relied on when she blamed the sickness of today's girls on LeRoy's very own brand of patriarchy, "the Jell-O curse," the great American company's history of oppression, itself a reflection of the culture that loved it. All women, she always said, are privy to a collective female unconscious. The girls in LeRoy suffered in particular, she believed, because they lived beneath the weight of an insular and conservative community, one that was itself colored by Jell-O, which was itself cursed by its complicity in conforming and molding women. Today's Jell-O girls "have been transformed into a theater for forgotten scenes." They express in the present the repression of the past. They embody the disappointment of a life in which satisfaction stems wholly from a well-manicured lawn, a well-manicured hand, well-behaved children; checking and savings accounts well balanced and safe; a perfect Jell-O salad, so light and clean and wholesome.

But all is not lost! At least not for Cixous and Clément, who write that hope and healing stem from the sorceress, "who in the end is able to dream nature and therefore conceive it, [who] incarnates the reinscription of the traces of paganism that triumphant Christianity repressed."

The traces of paganism. The traces of witchcraft. My mother the sorceress, who filled her art with goddess figures, feminine forms. Life-sized stained-glass windows of fleshy women seated meditatively in astral landscapes, or giving birth in verdant forests and overflowing streams. These were our protectors, she told me when I was a child: these were the women who would keep us healthy, keep us safe, free us from the curse.

27

My mother's wound ran like a cavern, pink and bottomless, down the length of her torso. It seemed to wait, embodied, for the constant care it demanded, like a child. Sterilization and wound packing. Drainage of the viscous yellow pus it secreted, a process performed by a thick tube attached to a bag my mother let flop at her side like an old-fashioned pocketbook. Because of the wound's proximity to her thin and damaged intestine, Mary was no longer allowed to eat. She would be fed, it was decided, via TPN, a permanent IV that would pump thousands of liquid calories into a central PICC line in her arm.

The wound was part of my mother, but we hated it. We knew if it became infected, she would die within days. So Judy and I tended to it like an undetonated bomb, donning masks and gloves, peeling open packets of sterile gauze and swabs we folded, like linens, into the basket of my mother's open belly. The skin inside descended in shades of pink toward her internal organs, and I was every time amazed by what I could see of her, how I could look inside her like a clock and find what made her tick. Judy and I performed each step with precision, chatting all the while to distract my mother, who glazed over as we worked. She could feel us inside her, she said, but there was no pain.

After the saline and gauze came the corseted bandage, which adhered to the skin on either side of the wound and laced up the middle, stitching up and tying off in bows the area of the incision, which formed a thick mound when covered over by layers of dressings and wads of sterile gauze. We bought yards of colored ribbon to replace the medical shoelace it came with, and cinched the corset with baby blue, rose-petal pink, polka dots, and glitter, all of us giggling as Judy and I threaded the baby blue through the bandage and primped and patted the neat package it made.

As the wound healed and food was reintroduced, new catastrophes arose. The weeks blurred with them, and emergency became the norm. We lived around it, in a constant state of numbness and flight. Of principal concern was my mother's "short gut syndrome," a complication of her bowel resection, characterized by chronic diarrhea and compounded by the removal of her TPN PICC line, which had threatened infection. Without supplemental nutrition and because of the diarrhea, my mother shrank, became bobble-headed and skeletal. The gastroenterologist told us that her body was now eating the thin layer of muscle between her forehead skin and skull. "This is what happens with people who are starving to death," she said.

"But she's been eating everything," we said, and by that point, it was true. Although she didn't always want to, my mother was devouring three times the amount of food she might otherwise consume. Brownies and beef. A whole bag of chips. Anything she wanted without the guilt. The irony was lost on no one. "Careful what you wish for," Mary said when I returned from the store with mountains of food, diapers, hemorrhoid cream.

Mary may have escaped the guilt of her gluttony, but I didn't. I felt guilty about everything: the extra hour I slept in, avoiding her care. The food I ate by her bedside, a necessity that felt phony, a performance designed to show her the self-care I was taking. I felt guilty for feeling annoyed by her neediness, which weighed upon me. Some days, I regarded her as my unwanted child. I felt guilty about how badly I wanted to escape her, as if her illness were my illness and I could outrun it. I imagined packing up my car and leaving. I daydreamed of an open road stretched before me, with California at its end, all pink and blue and desert brown. I dreamed of books and words. I wanted a story of my own and resented her illness for rewriting mine.

I had applied to MFA programs out west the previous winter, just before the back surgery, long before I knew of all the complications to follow. When I received the acceptance letters, knee-deep in medical crisis management, I'd already decided not to go. But I drove her to appointments and imagined how I might keep my foot on the gas all the way to the West Coast. A part of me relished the catastrophes I'd create in doing so, the fantasy tempered by the knowledge that I never would. Instead, I drove Mary to radiology, where a new, more permanent PICC line was implanted. They were going to try to bring her weight up, to keep her alive. The Hickman PICC bypassed Mary's arm veins and fed into the jugular vein that ran down her neck, twin lumens dangling from just below her left collarbone, two tassel-like lines to her heart. After its placement, you could see the silhouette of the line where it snaked along just underneath the skin.

My decision to stay and caretake was settled, I thought. But Mary insisted it wasn't. "Absolutely not," she said. "You're going to CalArts, and I'm going to help you move." She was splayed on the couch, TPN pumping away. She was already gaining weight. Her cheeks were rosy. Judy was in the chair beside her. "Oh, you're *going,*" she said. The TV was muted in the background.

"I am?" I said as Mary reached for the remote.

The two women nodded in unison, almost casually. My mother unmuted the TV because Jon Stewart was starting, and there would be no more discussion.

In the end, I went to California. Because Mary and Judy willed it. Because I did, too. In the end I took my mother with me, because Judy had gone to Florida and the wound still needed dressing, but also because, more than anything, she wanted to help me settle. She wanted to return to mothering me, and I wanted to let her. "I just need to know you'll be all right," she kept saying as she rushed to heal, to ready herself for the road I'd dreamed.

Each evening of our road trip, she lay on her back on a queen-sized motel bed and watched as I set out the sterile sheets, the tape and alcohol, the saline and Q-tipped sticks, before washing my hands for the third time in three minutes, returning and unwrapping another set of sterile gloves. The wound closed further each day, the skin around it sealing onto itself until eventually only a teardrop-sized spot of unclosed skin remained. Into this hole I shoved wads of saline-soaked gauze, sterile swabs, and Betadine-brown Q-tips. I did this until, eventually, no amount of force could insert the Q-tip into the hole, the last little space of open wound set just below her sternum. We whooped with joy that night, Mary sitting up on the edge of the bed, looking quizzically at her torso while I jumped up and down, chanting *Magical Mommy.*

Still, there were bad days, days when she slept for hours in the passenger seat, then woke suddenly, pulling on my sleeve to stop at the nearest toilet. "You shouldn't have come," I said to her one night after a particularly trying drive. "I needed to," she said. "I need to see the Grand Canyon." As a girl, she said, she'd gone with her parents, ridden a mule to the very center of the earth, watching the back of her mother's head as they descended into the coral chasm. She'd always wanted to return, but for some reason, she hadn't, not even on that camping trip with my father and me. So we took a long way through Arizona to spend a night there. "It will be the most beautiful thing you've ever seen," she kept saying as we drew nearer, promising us both.

We arrived with the sunset. She stood on the very edge, leaning on her cane, looking out over the open walls, the revealing shades of pink and veiny lines of white threaded over bare rock. When I came to stand beside her, we teetered, side by side, looking into the cavity of a body we both knew.

We passed into California the next day at dusk, crossing the state line with the sun going down behind plots of land peppered with cacti and Joshua trees. By nine we'd found the apartment Judy and I had rented, fully furnished and for too much money, over the phone just weeks before. We slept deeply in my new bed that night, each curled on our separate side.

The next day we bought plants for my

little patio. The day after we found the closest spot for a good walk. By the time she left, flying back to Connecticut, where she'd be on her own, the wound had fully closed, leaving only a thick strip of knotted skin running down the length of her torso. "Good-bye, my darling," she said as she climbed from the car. And then she was gone, and I was without her. And then I set about learning how to be alone.

As the months passed, I met friends, went to class, practiced yoga every evening. I wrote. I met Jon, who, six years later, would become my husband. From the center of my bed, I closed my eyes and listened for the horn of the late-night train, which called to me as it had when I was a child in that house by the water, falling into dreams in the blue bedroom my parents built for me. I felt safe in California. Safe enough to feel the fear I couldn't embody in the thick of my mother's illness. Without her, it was as if all the concern I had for her body transferred magically to my own. I thought of my physical self as delicate and unpredictable, preparing to fail. I saw the potential for unexpected death everywhere. I imagined earthquakes cracking the ground, opening cavernous holes to swallow me whole. I drove down the 405 picturing the scene of an accident I hadn't yet had, how my blood might splatter and stain. I imagined tumors, threats, heart attacks. The more I thought of this, the more my vision blurred and blinded me. Migraines arrived for the first time in my life. At a routine dental appointment, the dentist said my teeth were worn to stubs from clenching and grinding in the night. "I've never seen it so bad in someone your age," he told me. "You need to relax."

"I'm trying," I insisted, defensive. He looked skeptical, as if I were willfully diminishing myself. "I'm not crazy," I told him.

"I know," he said, sounding dubious.

But I believed myself. In survival mode, that was all that mattered. For all the catastrophe I imagined befalling me, I knew it was always imminent. I understood what other people didn't. For this I refused to apologize. I still refuse. I think of my mother, apologetic for her body, embarrassed by its short gut, the lumens and ports it bore, a cyborg's appendages. She so often saw her body as a failure. When cancer came she saw her physicality as cursed; when my father's affair began, she saw it as excessive, too busty or curvy, too scarred to please him. Her body rarely fit the narrow category that culture had assigned to it. But to me it was always magical: I came from it. I watched it sicken and survive, heal despite complications, deep wounds. Later I watched it die. And every process was beautiful.

Somehow, two years passed. Mary's tumors stayed small and symptom-free; my headaches disappeared. But when Jon and I moved to Texas and I started a PhD program, they began again. "No wonder," my mother said. "It's all about place."

I called her one afternoon in May. It was a hundred degrees outside already, and I'd just climbed in the car after an hour in the sun. I propped the phone between my chin and my ear, waiting for her answer, adjusting the air-conditioning to blow on my face, burning fever hot like moonstone, from the inside out. She picked up, and we talked about her friend who was in hospice. "She's dying," my mother said. She sounded confused, and I could hear her breath, short and labored and one thousand miles away. I was driving by then, asking for details through the wire of my headphones. But then I began noticing the skin of my left cheekbone, how it felt tired and shocked, as if stung. Soon, this feeling spread into my ear, down around my jaw. My heart began palpitating. I said nothing and considered driving myself to the emergency room. But I ended the call instead. "I should go," I said. "It's not safe." She agreed, and I was grateful. I didn't want to let on that I knew I was in trouble, and I didn't want her to tell me to get help, then worry when I put it off.

At home I looked up my symptoms online, convinced I was going to have a heart attack or a stroke. *I'll go to the doctor,* I told myself. I wrote myself notes. *Make an appointment,* they said, with *seriously, do it* in parentheses. But I was frightened, scared perhaps that I'd go and something *would* be wrong. I was scared that it would be my fault, the result of negligence, too much sugar-free Jell-O during my college days, or a history of illness, patterned on my insides. I was scared, too, that I would go and be told it was nothing; scared to then push and pressure, become *bitchy* and *hysterical* the way I knew I'd need to, to save myself.

Weeks passed. And then one day, Jon and I were side by side at the Houston gay pride parade when I saw splotches and felt faint. We returned to the car and started home.

"You're dehydrated," he said.

"I need you to take me" was all I could say. "I need you to take me." He held my hand as he steered the car, repeating *heat exhaustion.*

"Hold on hold on hold on," he said, his face blanched, unsure of what to make of my behavior. I was sobbing, doubled over in the passenger seat. In our six years together, he'd never seen me this way.

"My heart is exploding," I told him, and I meant it. I was rubbing my face and arms, trying to press them into feeling, but they were numb, immobile while the rest of me shook. "I'm going to die," I said.

"Hold on," he kept repeating, his words heavy, weighing me down. He pulled up outside the emergency room door, and I got out while he circled around to park. Inside I joined the line to have my vitals taken. The shaking worsened, and I wrapped my arms around myself to mask it, to make it to my chair.

In a thinly curtained exam room, a young doctor took my vitals, pressed cold EKG nodes onto my clammy skin. "You look healthy to me," she said while the machine ticked and worked, printing out the rhythm of my heart in peaks and valleys. "Normal as can be," she told me. She glanced at the page. "You're having a panic attack," she said. "This is how it usually happens for women, out of nowhere." I left the room feeling foolish.

But a year later, I pushed my way into a cardiologist's office because the palpitations weren't subsiding, only to learn that the panic attack probably *was* a panic attack but also a symptom of a physical abnormality of my heart, something invisible to an EKG. "Nothing too serious," the cardiologist said after I ran on a treadmill, lay naked on a table while she rubbed cold ultrasound gel on my chest. "But now you know where the palpitations come from." Now I know. She told me it's not uncommon for symptoms of this heart issue to be misdiagnosed as panic and anxiety disorders.

"But," she added, "it's also not uncommon for people with this condition to *have* panic and anxiety disorders."

"Why is that?" I asked her, and she shook her head. "We honestly don't know," she said. "It's just a documented symptom." The line, she suggested, between the body and the mind is a watery one. But I knew that already.

BOOK III

28

After every potential cause and contaminant had been exhausted, after blood draws and EKGs and X-rays all showed no physical abnormality, DENT Institute doctors issued the LeRoy girls a diagnosis: conversion disorder and mass psychogenic illness.

Conversion disorder, the doctors explained, is the literal transformation of emotional stress into physical symptoms. It's an enmeshment of the body and the mind, the involuntary and voluntary. Inside the brains of patients with conversion disorder, voluntary neural pathways light up, but the physical behavior these pathways prompt is experienced as involuntary. It's really quite common, lead doctors McVige and Mechtler explained — we see it all the time. Conversion disorder can be as simple as the stress headache one gets before visiting a troublesome in-law.

Mass psychogenic illness, however, is what

happens when physical symptoms spread for no physically apparent reason, most often through groups of young women. Scientifically, MPI remains a mystery. But every year some high school somewhere is struck by an MPI outbreak, although seldom for a prolonged period of time, as was the case in LeRoy. Also unusual about the case in LeRoy was the history of severe stress and trauma in the girls' backgrounds, which is rare for those who suffer from MPI, but not for those suffering from conversion disorder. MPI, it turns out, isn't common among trauma survivors, and I wonder if this is perhaps because, busy coping with their own pain, they have less immediate capacity to empathize with the pain of others.

Certainly I have known this to be true. Once, the sudden loss of my parents' marriage, the sudden loss of the only reality I'd known, produced in me a pain so hot, I froze my body to keep from burning. Icebound and blue, I was unable to feel anything, for anyone, including myself. Later, thawed and giving care, I worked to stay sensitive to my mother's plight. But even then there was only so much I could bear. To feel deeply for her would be to paralyze myself, and she needed me to stay capable and strong. So I learned, as I had during my adolescence, to power through the trauma like a robot, and save the feeling part for later. Even so, during my years as a caretaker, stress crept in. Before Mary's illness, I was iron-gutted, headache-free. But in the final years of her life, migraines arrived like storms, bringing nausea and vomiting, the need for silent darkness. It was as if I were returning to the nightmares of my girlhood, visiting the darkness to prepare myself for a world without my mother. The panic attack that sent me to the emergency room convinced me I was facing death, perhaps so my mother wouldn't have to. Twice in her final months I fainted, waking both times to Jon standing over me, yelling and shaking my shoulders. The first time I passed out, I hit my head in the shower. I woke to Jon, and a trail of blood running thin and pink down the drain, from the gash made where my head hit the porcelain.

A day later I went to my mother's primary care doctor to show her the cut and announce I was sure it was cancer, rare and hidden inside me, that was causing these sudden blackouts. Or maybe, I offered, the heart condition I'd been assured was benign was, in fact, serious. The cardiologist had called it congenital, but why, then, I wanted to know, was I only recently experiencing symptoms? My mother's doctor sighed, cleaned the cut. "We'll do bloodwork," she said. "And I'll order an EEG if you'd like, but honestly I think you're just taking on your mom's illness here a little." When the results came back normal, she wrote a script for Valium. "You really should talk to someone," she said. My diagnosis? Conversion disorder. The conversion of stress, preemptive grief, the intolerable sight of my mother's condition, into my own body, my own symptoms.

"I think that most girls are naturally empathetic," my mother said when we first discussed the outbreak in LeRoy. She was speaking of what is arguably the oddest feature of MPI: its predominance among women. Auguste Fabre would have said it's in our nature, something uncontrolled inside us, something in need of taming. Scientists today say it's a mystery, although my mother said she understood.

I laughed. "That's called essentialism," I said, putting on my haughty academic hat.

"What is?"

"Nothing," I said, taking the hat off

because, truth was, I admired my mother's essentialism, even if I knew it was dangerous or, in academic parlance, "problematic."

Given the psychic transference of symptoms through space and time that my mother said is natural to most women, it made sense to her that the lives of the girls of LeRoy were inextricably bound to the women in her family, who were themselves sick and bound to Jell-O, to what became of LeRoy without it. If we could speak to each other through our bodies, my mother reasoned, share stories through symptoms, perhaps we could pass down history as well. So she pictured whole generations of women, their struggles for freedom and escape, written like recipes on the genes they passed down, one woman to her daughter, and so on. The girls of LeRoy were reacting to violence and loss and oppression not only in their own lives, not only in each other's lives, but in their mothers' and grandmothers' lives as well. We are all connected, we women, we Jell-O girls, bound by a web of common experience, a common language we express through our bodies before we learn it is safe to speak.

Patriarchy is how the underbelly, the vampire side, the group hysteria, evolves, my mother wrote in 2012, the summer she found out about the girls. That summer, she began sending me clippings by mail and links by email, a constant stream of her own observations and analyses — as if, on top of being her caretaker, I was to be her documentarian, a living record of her enthrallment with these girls. In that first package, she'd sent me her copy of the *New York Times Magazine* feature and a handwritten letter on legal paper, her graceful cursive hemmed across the yellow page. *It's all connected,* she wrote, *the misogynistic temperature in LeRoy is high.* When the town let Ingham fail, she wrote, when they invested in Jell-O instead, they solidified the patriarchal legacy they live out today. She signed off by writing: *Remember, this stuff has been given to us for a reason; it presents us with the possibility of becoming more conscious. This is all part of our story.*

My mother understood MPI as a condition of the empathetic and therefore a condition to which women were especially susceptible. Scientifically speaking, her theory makes some sense, particularly when placed alongside other phenomenological "mirroring" behaviors such as yawning or menstrual synchrony. But like so many of my mother's arguments about women, her claim that we are *naturally* more empathetic than men breaks down in study after study, most of which identify difference, but none of which can parse nature from nurture.

Regardless of their gender, patients experiencing sympathy pain, phantom pain, pain with no discernible medical cause, arrive in doctors' offices on a daily basis. Large-scale MPI outbreaks, wherein the affected patients are numerous, are less common. But for DENT Institute doctors McVige and Mechtler, the diagnosis for the girls of LeRoy was obvious. Although MPI is rare, LeRoy is just the sort of insulated community in which it most often manifests. Salem, too, with its puritanical charter as a perfect society, *a city on a hill,* was ripe for conversion symptoms and their psychogenic spread. But it can be hard to believe what we cannot see, and harder still to understand a phenomenon in which multiple people inexplicably and involuntarily develop identical physical symptoms with no discernible physical cause. So just as the people of Salem searched for the devil, the girls and their parents, the town of LeRoy, searched for contaminants — barrels of waste, chemical-laced cafeteria food, airborne infections — something to explain what confused and frightened them. They searched, too, for authority, for someone with knowledge to tell them what the problem was and to give them an answer they wanted to hear.

After the diagnosis from DENT, many parents in LeRoy pushed back, refusing to believe their daughters' "mystery illness" could be emotional. It must instead be environmental, they said, the result of something toxic, something inherent in the town that was making the girls sick. When I heard this, I thought of Oatka Creek, how it ran red, orange, and yellow with sweet chemicals for years. How charming this story seems at first blush, quaint somehow, but dark underneath, Jell-O waste, a poison to the town's central artery.

In February 2012 a panel of school officials and environmental experts sat at a long table in the school auditorium and fielded angry questions from a crowd of parents. Katie Krautwurst's mother had contacted famed environmental activist Erin Brockovich about the town's potential contamination by a 1970 train derailment, and Brockovich had flown in, brightening the anxious media spotlight on the town. The EPA subsequently became involved but quickly determined there were no contaminants in the majority of the soil that had been affected by the train disaster, sealed off in drums and kept on site in LeRoy. (They only tested 203 of the 235 drums, however; the other thirty-two drums remain unspoken for but were sent to a toxic-waste removal site in Michigan.) The site of the Jell-O factory, and Oatka Creek, into which it once pumped refuse, went untested.

Not surprisingly, conspiracy blogs spouting theories of government cover-ups, and superficial news articles accentuating the mystery of the girls, cropped up. The town fell into a media-saturated malaise marked by confusion and contradiction, an environment that was universally detrimental to the girls' condition, which worsened with each news story published. The rumors of toxic-waste spills and chemicals left behind when manufacturing abandoned the town still ran rampant, even after months of testing. Footage of the meeting, featured prominently on local news reports and immortalized now on the internet, shows parents pointing fingers like pitchforks at school superintendent Kim Cox. "You are not doing your job at all," one woman yells. The crowd applauds.

The visible, angry fear of that meeting stemmed in part from the fact that for weeks preceding it, letters had been arriving by the boxful on Cox's desk. In them, everything from poisoning to possession to malingering was proposed — but of all these theories, the most popular was that the girls had all smoked the same synthetic marijuana just before their symptoms began. Synthetic marijuana, also known as spice and K2, was legal and unregulated at the time, although it has since been banned in New York State. Much in the same way that accusations of malingering suggested that the girls themselves were to blame for their condition, rumors that synthetic pot was to blame for the outbreak insinuated that these girls were bad girls, a tale the American media still loves to tell. A tale that also performs a common societal tic: we tend to blame the female body for the array of collective anxieties it's often saddled with. We tend to think that when a woman expresses her bodily pain or suffering, her very expression of it is also her crime. She is both perpetrator and victim of her own trauma. But in doing so we cover over the complicated truth of our anxieties, placing them instead inside the image of a woman, a girl, making her a vessel for all our fears.

29

Many years ago now, after my mother and I visited LeRoy for Jell-O's hundredth-anniversary party, after we scraped moss from Midge's overgrown grave, Mary found herself distressed by the state of her mother's headstone. She hadn't yet left my father then, and we returned to the dark house in New Hampshire, where the grave remained all she could think about, as if in her absence the ground would swallow up the stone, taking with it the world's memory of Midge. My mother had fought hard to hold on to her memories of her mother, and even so, she sometimes felt like Midge had been a figment of her imagination. This feeling washed over her in unpredictable waves, and she would respond by spending afternoons hunched over the binders she kept of her mother's letters, closing her eyes to try to hear Midge's voice.

Even when she found it, an echo of

Midge's soft tone in her distant mind, she still fixated on the headstone. And so she decided to make a new stone, a better stone, one more suited to her mother's true character. Together, we drove to a quarry and walked through rows of granite, looking for the perfect marker, something small but sturdy, a subdued gray, like Midge herself, but threaded with traces of pink to keep it warm, to show her heart. When we found it, when the stone was finished, Midge's handwriting, *Mary Jane Fussell,* laced across the granite, as if she herself had signed her approval.

My mother, father, and I drove the stone to LeRoy in the early summer, less than a year before she'd move to Vermont. There, we gathered with Tom and his wife and children at the cemetery for a ceremony — insisted upon by my mother — for which only she and I dressed up. Tom's wife and I awkwardly sang "Amazing Grace," everyone else staring solemnly at the new stone. At the time I couldn't tell why this was a big deal to my mother. Tom and my father seemed equally clueless. But she wept as we sang, and as we drove away, as if she were leaving her mother all over again. She was disappointed, she said, that it hadn't gone the way she'd planned. "What did you expect to happen?" I asked. She took my hand and squeezed. "Oh, I don't know," she sighed, wiping her tears with the sad resignation of a woman who'd spent most of her life trying to know a ghost.

I wonder now if it was on that trip that my mother realized she'd never return to LeRoy. Perhaps she knew that her relationship with Tom had reached a natural end point. Perhaps she understood, once and for all, that Midge wasn't there in the ground, not really. Midge was in her memory, in her *memwah,* and in me.

Even so, she kept Midge's old gravestone, which weighed down the back of our car as we drove home to the woods, where she put it in the garden. Nine months later, when she left George for her farmhouse in Vermont, she took it with her. In 2004, when she moved back to Connecticut, it came along, and my mother, knowing somehow that this would be her last home, had it built into a stone wall, where it remains.

The year my mother returned to Connecticut, shortly after her first liver resection, and midway through my freshman year of college, she proposed that Aunt Edith's trust, money she and Tom shared, be split between them. She had always felt shackled to the money, to LeRoy and Jell-O; and to Tom, with whom she'd barely spoken since the gravestone ceremony. She was tired, she said, of maintaining a relationship dependent on how closely she adhered to Tom's ideas of normality, propriety, a *productive* life. A life like his, which is a LeRoy life, a life of the law, his practice on Main Street, his house modest enough to hide his fortune, his wife and children, the shiny matching Buicks parked in the drive.

But at first all she would say was "We have different investment goals," unwilling to admit what she really wanted was freedom from Tom, and from the big bank, its corporate management policy, each portfolio the same. She had found a money manager in Vermont she liked, but without the split she couldn't move her share. They ended up in a lawsuit. There were questions about how the trust should be split and how it should be managed, but, most hurtful, there were statements and arguments from Tom in which he appeared to reveal a lifetime of feelings — loss and anger and betrayal. Mary, he indicated, was irresponsible and wasteful. She had never been normal. It was no wonder she'd wound up in a mental hospital. As an adult she had chosen the life of a *starving artist* but had spoiled me, her only child, by sending me to private schools. *His* children had gone to public school in LeRoy. They were hardworking. They had families to support. And anyway, Aunt Edith never trusted Mary; although she had set up the trust when Mary was five, she could already tell her young niece was *dramatic.*

While the court ruled first in favor of my mother, the ruling was overturned on appeal. The final verdict preserved the shared trust but proclaimed that should Mary die first, the trust would end, splitting in half between me, her only heir, and Tom. If not, the trust would divide four ways, between my mother (and later me), and Tom's three children.

By that point it didn't matter to Mary. She was exhausted by the expense of the lawsuit and the meanness of Tom's words. She didn't want to talk to him again, she said, not in anger, but in sad resignation. "It was deeply hurtful," she said any time I asked, "the culmination of a lifetime of conflict. I just couldn't take any more." Her only regret, she said, was never again seeing her mother's grave. "Just to check in on her," she said. "But I've made peace with it, I've let all that go."

I wondered if that was true. Already she

was slipping away. Even if I didn't know it yet, I sensed it. And though in 2014 I asked my graduate program in Texas for money to visit LeRoy and research the girls, what I really wanted was to visit Midge's grave, as if my body could serve as an avatar for my mother's, bringing her closer to her mother and giving her the peace she needed to travel fearlessly toward death.

I'd tried several times to reach the LeRoy girls, but since the article in the *Times* magazine, they've vanished from the public sphere, guarded by mothers who've had it with the media attention that was only making their daughters sicker. Did I want to contribute to their illness? Did I want to be part of the problem? I did not. But I did want to be close to them, to stand in the town center, shut my eyes and see if I felt whatever had pulsed inside them, whatever trauma they'd shared; I wanted to see if I shared it, too, trauma or memory, the feeling of my grandmother's ghost, assuring me there was something more, something beyond the physical, something I might reach for when my mother's body passed away.

So that summer, when my mother was still well enough to walk around her garden, planning the wedding Jon and I would have there in a year's time, I wrote to Tom, saying I was interested in our family history. "Visit anytime," he said, and so we did — Jon and I borrowing my mother's car, backing from her driveway while she waved at us from behind the red garden gate. "Go find out what happened," she called, but I just waved, hoping I'd return with the knowledge she craved, fearing I wouldn't.

We drove north for hours before cutting up into the Berkshires. It was early July, and the landscape grew up around us in mountains of verdancy. We passed by Stockbridge and pulled off the highway to drive through Riggs. We stopped in Rochester for coffee with Marcia, Mary's childhood friend. By the time we reached LeRoy, the sky was blue and dusky, the bugs were emerging.

We drove in on a two-lane road, the gray pavement carrying us through green fields that dissipated over time, changing to small plots with little houses on them, little front yards ornamented with windmills and birdbaths and American flags. When we hit the edge of town, a sign welcomed us: *Welcome to LeRoy, Birthplace of Jell-O.* We slowed down for Main Street, which looked, on the surface at least, exactly as I remembered it. I had imagined total dilapidation. But the storefronts that remained were well kept.

We passed the Woodward Library, dipped over a hill across the railroad tracks, to the Jell-O factory. We pulled in, parked the car, and got out, holding our hands up to our foreheads to squint at the building's disrepair. In the front were offices, or maybe just storage rooms, of a company whose purpose I couldn't make out. But the back of the building, the factory itself, was empty and paint splattered, used from time to time for paintball battles. The lawn was grassy and unkempt, hemmed in by a fence separating the factory land from the short lawn of the town cemetery. At first I couldn't believe the two locations were so closely linked. I hadn't remembered them this way. But it seemed somehow fitting, and I wedged my toes into the fence and stood up taller so that I could see across the sea of stones to the Woodward Mausoleum, imposing gray with columns and stained-glass windows. I squinted, scanning for Midge's headstone, although I knew it was small, tucked somewhere away from the Woodwards, somewhere I'd forgotten entirely.

Jon called to me, and I walked over to where he was standing, and, on my tiptoes, peered into a broken window. He helped me up onto a pile of rocks outside it, and I tried and failed to fit myself around the shattered pane and into the building. With just my head poking through the sharp circle of broken glass, I squinted at the tiled floor, the industrial lamps hung from taut wire, all of it brightened by the dusky sunlight cutting through the windows in thin squares, like pages of light. For a moment, I wanted to curl inside their warmth and never leave, but the feeling passed away. "Oh well," I said, stepping backward carefully, over the rubble, to solid ground. I felt relieved, then guilty when I landed, as if I should persist, should draw blood breaking through the glass and crawling past its jagged edges. I thought of the LeRoy girls, so close by. I imagined finding their homes and knocking on their doors, fighting my way inside, as if I could force my way into their stories to better know my own. Was that what I should be doing?

The air-conditioning in our hotel room that night rattled and died over and over, and still I slept heavily, burdened by dreams I couldn't remember. We woke tired, itchy-eyed, and I sprang out of bed, worried we'd be late to meet Tom, who was expecting us at ten. I'd told him my terms for the day, what I'd like to do. I didn't want to wind up sitting on his sofa making awkward conversation. Instead I wanted to go to the Jell-O museum, but mostly I wanted to go to the cemetery.

Tom's house was exactly as I'd remembered it, matching Buicks and all. He welcomed us with stiff hugs, and then we left, driving first to the museum. Tom rode in the front seat of our car, issuing directions. We passed over the bridge, and I mentioned Main Street. "It looks just like I remembered it," I said, noting that, compared with many places, LeRoy still seemed prosperous. "But things aren't good," Tom said quickly, speaking then about the loss of the factory work that once drove the town. "Many of the houses along Main Street are rentals now," he said. "Nothing is kept up the way it used to be." I realized then that the changes to LeRoy I'd read about have taken place over many years; a slow fade, a disintegration from the inside out. I imagined how the town must have looked at its best, every storefront filled, every resident working, the creek running Jell-O-sweet and colorful in the summer, solid and sure for every skater at Christmas-time. I imagined my mother and Tom, gliding over the crust of icy water, walking home in soggy coats and mittens, Tom all business, with his blades over one shoulder, his hands in his pockets, and my mother trailing along behind him, shaping snowballs and touching her tongue to their flavorless absence. Given this, given what my uncle must remember, it makes sense, the depressed emptiness he sees in the town now. But he's stayed.

We arrived at the Jell-O Museum, a one-room building full of framed advertisements and recipes. We took the short tour, then wandered around. Jon initiated a photograph, and Tom and I stood, stiff and smiling, against the archaic backdrop. Tom put one arm around my waist with a formality that belied only fear, and I felt suddenly awash with a tenderness I'd not imagined I could muster. Maybe it was something about the nearness of blood, the nearness of my mother; maybe it was simply that I felt sorry for him, estranged from her for so many years.

Afterward, we walked the Jell-O Brick Road from the museum to the LeRoy House, an old white colonial. Inside it was quiet and musty, the floors thick with oriental rugs, the walls lined with relics, including a life-sized portrait of my great-

great-aunt Edith wearing a blue silk dress and smiling like the *Mona Lisa*.

In the next room was a small exhibit, nothing more than a glass display box with a few waxy documents, a few images. But the box caught my eye, and I walked over to look closer. Inside was a drawing, tinted blue, of the town of LeRoy as it must have looked one hundred years before, bustling with horses and buggies, boaters on the creek, women with parasols waving to them from the bridge. And a campus, dormitories, and a library, all of it flanked by the words *Female seminary, Ingham University, 1876.* "Apparently there was a vote put to the people of LeRoy," Tom said, coming up behind us. "Bail out the school or let it sink." But the town did the latter, the school was leveled, and from the rubble the Woodwards built their own library, the etched capitals of their name erasing INGHAM for all time. Never in all my research about Jell-O and LeRoy, never even in my mother's writing, had I read that Ingham's closure boiled down to a town vote. Never had I known it was the town's decision.

Heavy, the weight of this history, so heavy that in the moment I had nothing to say, no adequate response. Now I wonder what would have changed in LeRoy if the rise of

Jell-O had somehow coincided with the rise of the country's first women's university. For a moment I imagine the dessert supporting the school, my family's wealth funneled into educating women outside the kitchen, the myriad ways to make the perfect pointless mold. All of this was a choice. Money and conformity over intellectualism and free thought. This choice was what my mother hated about LeRoy; perhaps this choice was what first cast the curse that kept LeRoy frozen in the patriarchal past.

In the car on the way to the cemetery to see Midge's grave, I sat in the backseat while Jon drove and Tom directed. For some reason I'd been nervous to ask about the girls, but I couldn't see my uncle's face, and this emboldened me. "So," I said, "what happened with the girls a few years back?"

"Oh," he said, rearranging in his seat. The moment felt pivotal, and I realized I'd expected him to deny the whole thing, to call the girls hysterical, to accuse them of the emotional problems he'd charged my mother with. But now I was suddenly unsure of what he'd say. I pulled my phone out of my purse and recorded him without asking, so I wouldn't forget his answer, but

I fumbled with the buttons and botched the whole thing. The resultant audio is short and foggy, rising and falling with Tom's nasal upstate accent:

"As I understand it," he says, "— turn left here — there had been a girl at the high school who had kind of Tourette's syndrome. Well, she was a popular girl, and everybody thought very" — he pauses — "very highly of her, and the theory seems to be she was a role model for these other girls, and it was kind of a, if one does it then another one does it then another one does it, and I think it was kind of proven to be true because all the girls that got therapy got better, overcame their . . . problems."

Their problems. Their *emotional problems.* What Tom referred to when he wrote that Mary *suffers from emotional problems that cause her to see the world unrealistically.* At the time I wondered what about the world was unrealistic through my mother's eyes. Was it simply that she believed she should be allowed to control her own money? Was this an unrealistic request? I imagined what my father would have said if he'd read the letter, how he might have agreed, asserting once again that my mother had imagined his affair, telling me the same if I dared to question him. It was my mother's emotions that were to blame for my parents' divorce, he asserted time and again, not his own actions.

Given this sort of rhetoric, it's no surprise that in the small, conservative town they lived in, in the larger misogynistic culture they lived in, emotion was indeed a problem for the girls of LeRoy. So, like generations of women before them, they tried to block out their feelings and ignore their pain. But it had to come out eventually, didn't it?

As Tom spoke of the girls and their *problems,* I thought about my mother as a child, craning her neck to watch the Italian women mourn, rending their garments, shaking and screaming. I imagined her at Riggs, frozen before a panel of men issuing her diagnosis, informing her of her problems. What might have changed in Mary's life if she'd been allowed to speak her trauma and her loss in the first place? I wondered the same of Katie Krautwurst, Thera Sanchez, and myself; I imagined what might still change for us if we gave ourselves over to wandering through the dark forest of our grief. Could we trust ourselves to forge a path? Could we trust that we'd someday emerge?

Tom knew just where the grave was. When

we arrived, Midge's stone was smaller than I'd remembered. Where once her handwriting was crisp and new, now it had faded, her name indistinct. I felt suddenly panicked, realizing that I had to return to my mother with images of the faded stones. I'd meant my pilgrimage to LeRoy to be a healing journey, from which I would return bearing images of Midge's permanence, reassurance that when my mother went to meet her, she, too, would be remembered by those she left behind.

The three of us stood for a few moments, gazing at the stones. Then I took photos, knelt by Midge's headstone to scrape away moss, just as I had on that trip to LeRoy as a child. But within minutes there was nothing more to do. We shifted awkwardly, then returned to the car and drove back to Tom's house. In the driveway, we hugged again, and then Jon and I climbed back into our car and pulled in reverse away from my uncle.

"Tell me all about it," my mother said when we returned to her house after dark, exhausted from the drive, carrying our bags, our bodies drooping under the weight. I told her it was good, but couldn't think of what else to say, so I said, "I'll give you all the details later." She seemed disappointed. But she was tired, too, she told me, and by the time I'd showered, she'd changed into her nightgown and climbed into bed. While Jon made dinner downstairs, I knocked softly on her door, pushing it open just enough to see the light still on. She was reading, her knees little mountains beneath the covers, her dog under the bed, snoring, the cat settled in beside her, cleaning his face with his paws. There were several water glasses on her bedside table, her phone, an array of pill bottles. She rubbed her eyes, said again she was exhausted. She enunciated *ex-haaaaausted,* punctuating her *a*'s with little lurches. I climbed up beside her. "Want to hear about it?" I asked, and she nodded.

"He was in his element, I suppose," she said of Tom when I told her about the tour. She was quiet, expecting a climactic event, but I wasn't sure what else to say. "Did you go to the graveyard?" she asked. I told her we did and tried to avoid explaining how weather-beaten the headstone was. But she found out the next morning at the breakfast table, when I pulled up pictures on my phone. She was crestfallen at the sight of her mother's grave. "It looked better in person," I told her.

She spent the rest of the day in the studio,

writing. Jon and I were eating dinner when she came in, the screen door slamming behind her, the sound of dog's nails on the hardwood floor preceding her coming. "I put some writing together for you," she said, bending at the waist to lug a limp TPN bag from the fridge. She sighed. "It'll tell you everything you need to know." She patted the bag like a good dog. "Get nice and toasty," she said, addressing her dinner, which needed time to warm before she "hooked up." Too cold and it would freeze the thin membranes of her veins.

A month into autumn, after I'd returned to Texas for the fall semester, Mary called to confess she was losing weight again. "They're upping my weekly intake," she said, "no big deal." There was an edge to her voice. It remained each time we talked, a distraction in the background of our chatter, a distant vibration, like a radio playing on one speaker's side of the line. "What's that noise?" I wanted to say, but didn't, not for her sake but for mine.

I'd always called her often. "What's up?" she'd say. "Just chatting," I'd answer, and she'd say, "Oh good," and we'd settle in. I'd talk to her while I drove, did laundry, made dinner, made plans. She'd talk to me while she painted, walked the dogs, or skimmed the pages she'd written that day. But now when I called she answered in a muffled voice, as if just waking up. "I'm in bed," she said any time after five o'clock. At first I ignored the edge in her voice that grew each week after we left Connecticut. "It's the cold," she said when I finally asked. "It's the thought of another winter." By the time she admitted it was her body, the first snow had fallen. "I don't know what happened," she said, "but everything has gone to hell in a handbasket." The first CT scan revealed nothing, the second showed shadows, tumors drifting in again like clouds across the surface of her liver.

My mother had many times said, "This is the last time I will do this." She said so after trips and surgeries and marriage. She said so after too much time spent alone, too much time spent in the company of others. For the most part, she meant what she said when she decided never to do something again. I learned to trust her. But I suppose I should have known that her past pledges to never go under the knife again couldn't be taken seriously, not when spoken by painkillers and pain. And I suppose I should have considered that fear, the fear of doing nothing, would drive her to act, to undo her past decisions not to. She was not one to do nothing. I should have known all this, but I was still surprised when she told me about a surgery, another one, to remove her latest tumors. "Yale said it couldn't be done," she scoffed, "but I've found a liver specialist at Sinai who says he can make it work."

So Jon and Judy and I flew to New York a week before Christmas. The city was cold but dry. We prayed for snow. We waited for it to fall while we waited for her to survive surgery, which she did. The surgeon told us it was successful, told us he planned all weekend for the difficult maneuvering he did around the blood vessels onto which tumors had leeched themselves. He looked proud when he said "best possible outcome." Still, it was always all the same, surgery and recovery, my mother's sticky nightgowns, her matted hair; pumps and pill schedules and alcohol swabs; Jell-O and pink pitchers of water and juice; roommates who whined and wailed from behind curtains; the cold air to kill infections inside the hospital, the cold New York December outside.

30

After I left my mother and returned to Houston, the distance expanded, magnified. Before I'd always felt her body alive on the other side of the country, that energetic umbilical cord still tethering me. Now the connection felt weaker.

At Mount Sinai, there had been improvement but little resolution as we prepared to leave for Texas and a new semester I both looked forward to and dreaded. She was feeling worse, she said, shaking. She was short of breath, the result of fluid still stuck in the lungs, not pneumonic, not yet. *Walk, sit upright, cough it out, eat and drink, get your strength up,* the doctors ordered. She nodded obediently, ate little. The physical therapist arrived and had her stand, balancing on one foot, then the other. "This isn't hard for you, right?" he asked. She shook her head. When I left for the airport, they were marching in place, my mother's forehead furrowed, her gaze fixed on the unknowable distance in front of her.

From Houston, I called her daily, looking for reassurance. "Are you there?" I'd ask the machine if she didn't pick up. "Are you eating?"

"A little," she said when she answered, her breath heavy on her side of the line. I could tell she was lying, protecting me. By then she was alone again, Judy gone to her house in Florida.

"Well, who's helping you with groceries? Who's helping you walk the dogs?"

"I'm managing," my mother said, sounding a little affronted. "Your father," she added, to which I wasn't sure how to respond.

A year before the CT scan and the cloudy tumors, before the surgery, my father had arrived on her doorstep. All the way from New Hampshire to ask her if she'd like to take a dog walk. I picture him, in his Levis and his leather jacket, antsy at the threshold of her house. I picture him entering, greeting her dogs, spending too much time petting them to avoid the awkwardness of looking in her eyes. It had been so long, so many years, he said. But their daughter would be getting married soon, and wouldn't it be nice if they could celebrate the day together?

This, they'd both understood, would take time. So they'd returned to the autumn beach where they'd walked hand in hand twenty-seven years before. Two weeks later, he'd come again, and they'd walked again.

All of which scared me. I'd hungered for this for years, for the normalcy of parents who cared for each other. But now I was indignant. Why now? I wanted to know. Why only now, when I was settled in life and love? "We just weren't ready yet," my mother said. "We both had so much growing up to do."

After the surgery, after Judy and I left, as Mary's strength began to wane, my parents stopped walking and started driving, my father piloting them around for hours, making jokes, making sure they passed all their old haunts, and Mary watching from the passenger seat as the world whipped by.

She looked forward to these dates, she told me. Even depended on them a little. But it was me she called one morning in February, two months after the surgery. She couldn't stop vomiting, she said, her voice panicked and thin, and she didn't want to go to Yale.

"Okay," I said, switching into crisis management, "let's find a way to get you to Sinai."

"I was wondering," she said timidly, "I was wondering about asking your father."

I paused. "I think that's a good idea," I said. I could tell it scared her but also made her feel safe. She'd always wanted a man to save her, even after she'd learned she had to save herself.

I called my father before she did. "Absolutely," he said when I told him what was happening, and drove through the night to get to her.

Jon and I flew to New York. There was a new room, a new roommate. IV fluids to get her strength up, and the insertion of a G-tube, which fed from a hole in her side to her stomach, where it was designed to drain fluid before she could throw it up. The tube hooked to a bag that hung from the side of her bed, a clear pocketbook of bile. "It's all clogged up," I'd tell the nurses. Judy arrived and said the same thing. "It's working," they'd assure us. But anyone could see it wasn't. She was still vomiting. They tried a bigger hose. When it fell out, they put the old one back in. Eventually they sent her home. "Take it up with her gastroenterologist," they told us. "Ask her oncologist," they said. Judy and I sent emails, made calls, most of which received curt answers, if they were answered at all. Mary had been an interesting case two months before. Now everyone was retreating, a team of doctors suddenly childlike in their powerlessness, walking backwards on their tiptoes.

On Mary's birthday, Jon bought an inflatable crown and an array of balloons, boxes of black cherry Jell-O, and a can of Reddi-wip. Together we stirred the powder, watching it dissolve, then returning hours later to see if it had set. We poked the mold. It wiggled resiliently. Jon flipped it over onto a platter while I said, "Careful careful," shaking the mold to dislodge the perfect purple mass. We topped it with candles and a mountain of whipped cream, creating a comical mountain of sugar. "It's ready," we called to Judy and Richard, who gathered round the table, waiting while I fetched Mary, who leaned on my arm, entwined with hers, as we walked to the table. She sat like a queen in her crown and fluffy white bathrobe, clapping while we sang "Happy Birthday." Jon dolloped Jell-O onto everyone's plate, and we ate it, equal parts disgusted and delighted.

Later, alone in the kitchen, I couldn't stop picking at the leftover mold. I peeled back the Saran Wrap covering the Jell-O, poked a spoon in, and doled a little out, covering it back up as I went. It tasted tinny, like chemicals and red dye and the source of sickness. But I went back for more and didn't stop until the bowl was empty.

31

For 120 years, Jell-O has survived economic upheaval and cultural change. It has weathered the public-relations nightmares wrought by frat culture and Bill Cosby. It has shape-shifted from dessert, to salad, to diet food, to snack. But now it appears to face only decline. Outside of Utah, where Jell-O is the official state snack, sales are low. Perhaps it's only a matter of time before America's Favorite Dessert becomes a relic of the past.

I wonder if Jell-O's fate will ultimately have to do with what my mother hated about it: the brand's association with domestic science and 1950s suburbia. Jell-O isn't sexy, and it's certainly not healthy, both attributes of growing concern to a country knee-deep in dueling epidemics of obesity and celebrity. Even with the recent introduction of Simply Good, a small, "natural" line free of dyes and preservatives, Jell-O is, for many, now considered a grotesque junk food of the Spam variety, a far cry from the light and wholesome persona it owned for decades. Whereas once Jell-O's artificially bright colors and ability to contain a fridge full of leftovers were the draw, now blogs and BuzzFeed lists abound, chronicling the grossness of old recipes.

Jell-O may not be sexy, but making it can be a joyful affair. This according to Kraft's senior marketing director, who has recently announced that his team is currently at work rebranding Jell-O as a "fun food." When did we lose track of food for fun? he wants to know, although it remains unclear how much fun he considers the carcinogenic chemicals and dyes still featured in most Jell-O products.

I suppose Jell-O could be a fun food for some. But to me, despite the violence that has always made and marketed it, Jell-O is still all about caretaking. Mothers caring for husbands and children and entire congregations of potluck-goers; friends caring for each other; children caring for their parents; daughters and dieters — like me — caring for themselves by making the *delightfully lite* choice. In the twenty-first century, even men have gotten in on the action.

Corporate marketing's recent discovery of

stay-at-home dads and the consumer potential in this demographic is reflected by today's Jell-O commercials, several of which feature fathers and sons bonding over an after-work/after-school treat. In a 2013 spot for Jell-O pudding, a redheaded, apron-wearing dad greets his young redheaded son, who is fresh off the bus after the first day of school. "It'll be easier tomorrow," the dad assures him, passing his boy a bowl of chocolate pudding. "I have to go back?" his shocked son says, pausing midbite. "Better make it a double."

In another ad, an overweight, balding dad sits at the kitchen table with his son, swirling his spoon through a plastic cup of Jell-O while he describes how miserable the rest of his life is. Dead-end job, long commute, hair loss, the list goes on. Jell-O is the one bright spot in his day, he suggests. "You need this more than me," his son says, sliding his pudding cup across the table so that his father now has two desserts rather than one.

This particular motif of a child caring for a parent is constant in Jell-O's mythology over the decades. From the first appearance of the Jell-O girl herself — *So easy, even a child can do it* — and her penchant for surprising Mama, to a spot from the eighties in which a loving daughter makes her parents an orange Jell-O mold in the shape of fifty, the number of years they'd been married. And finally to my mother and me, slowly walking arm in arm toward the kitchen table, where a jiggling birthday mold waited, offering, inviting, the last meal she'd ever eat.

32

Two months after we left New York, Jon and I packed up the car in Texas and drove through days and nights and time zones, arriving in Connecticut on a clear spring night, smatterings of stars like tumors in the cold, dark sky. We'd talked the whole drive about the wedding we were planning for Mary and Judy's garden in June. A DIY affair with three days of camping for our friends in the back woods, and karaoke in the garden. "It'll just be a big party with a wedding attached," we said, not worrying that we still needed tents, catering, a dress for me, a ring for Jon.

The casual approach had been my idea, avoidant in a way. I'd never dreamed of marriage. A white meringue dress and a diamond always seemed a trap to me, and, like Mary and Midge, I dreamed of travel, freedom, roads stretching endlessly before me. But I dreamed, too, of Jon, a love strong and tender. I dreamed of him with such specificity, I sometimes think I conjured him. But we were good as we were, cohabitants for years by the time the wedding arrived. What would change with the exchange of rings? This question didn't seem to cross his mind. He wasn't worried, he said. But I imagined how I might fade within our marriage, become a woman too domestic to desire, dulled as if by magic the moment the ring slid onto my finger. I thought often of Midge and her writing, how quickly it had been abandoned to wifedom and motherhood, how she'd pined for the life she could have had. I thought of the drama teacher, how her power stemmed from her otherness, how in marriage I could never be my husband's other woman, and how that made me vulnerable to his betrayal. I thought, too, about the Jell-O money Jon would marry into, the way it had changed my parents' relationship, and how we might work together to escape their fate. I called my mother often to discuss. "You're different than I was," she insisted. "You know yourself better." The sureness in her voice was the sureness she brought to our conversations about the LeRoy girls and what happened to them. "No doubt in my mind," she'd say about the origins of their illness, and about my ability to avoid their fate.

"We'll set it all up together," my mother had said, "we'll make this wedding perfect for you." But when she answered the door, the night of our arrival, dogs milling around her, I lost my breath at the sight of her, her body halved since I'd seen her last, just a wooden doll composed of hinges, her face swollen as if stung. "Hi," she warbled, reaching out to hug us, and we hid our shock, held her close. But upstairs in my attic room, surrounded by my childhood things, I sobbed to Jon. "What will we do if she dies before June?" He swept my hair off my face, touched my cheek. "We'll have the wedding anyway," he said. For a moment, I felt repulsed, even as I myself had brought it up. How could he think of going through with our marriage on the heels of my mother's death? He was trying to comfort me, to tell me he'd hold me in her absence. But I couldn't imagine doing anything without her, let alone getting married. There were so many new roles I was about to assume. How could I fill them without her? How could I leave my twenties, become a wife, and cease to become her daughter? It seemed the world would stop with my mother's last breath. In a way, I wanted it to.

We slept deeply in her house, our small attic room cool and dark. We rose late, unsure of what to do. We wandered aimlessly around the backyard, pointing out places where we'd like to have this or that — a makeshift shower for the campers, a table for snacks. We took trips to Costco, reading to each other off crumpled lists. We hid out at the local Planet Fitness, having suddenly realized that we were not in wedding shape. In the backyard we built a campsite around the fire pit my mother had commissioned from her landscaper a month before, when she could still walk around outside, when doing so didn't drain her of everything she had. Now she stayed in bed all day, vomit bucket within reach, curtains open, gazing at the garden she remembered Judy planting thirty years before, blooming in yellow and blue. "There were always parties in this house," she said when I climbed in bed with her one night. "Remember," she said, "we cut flowers for bouquets, shucked corn on the back porch." We danced sprinkler dances, jumping through the waving fan of water, kaleidoscopic in the afternoon light. I remember.

"Tell me what you think of this dress," I said, changing the subject, thumping up the attic stairs outside her room and returning with the latest of my online shopping efforts, a wispy cream-colored gown with a skirt that swept the floor, and a simple low V-neckline. "It's very revealing," she said critically when I put it on for her. "But then, what do I know?" she said when she saw my disappointment. "I wore a winter coat when I married your dad."

"It's okay," I told her, but climbed the stairs back to my room feeling miffed, feeling I should wear whatever I wanted to my wedding, set the tone early on for the freedom I wanted my marriage to embody. Feeling my mother should understand the desire for freedom more than anyone. But freedom was hard to conjure in those days, the house like a capsule in which we lived, waiting for marriage, waiting for death.

"I just can't stand it," Mary would say when the waves arose again, sweeping over her as she retched for long minutes, her empty body trying to empty itself further. When finally she agreed to the hospital, it was a relief to know she was there, safe. Jon and I visited daily, cued up our first-dance song on his iPhone and practiced our Texas two-step for her in the cramped, curtained room. She closed her cotton mouth over a smile, placed her palms together in silent applause. "You two," she said, miming the A-okay sign.

My father visited when he could, all the way from New Hampshire, to stand by her bedside and rearrange the flowers he brought because, she said, "they're fighting."

"They're friendly now," he said, kissing her forehead, and all I could think was that for years he couldn't say her name.

A few weeks before the wedding, a palliative care nurse named Ursula pulled me into the hallway to discuss *hospice options.* But I brushed her off, said I'd think about it, and returned to the room indignant that she'd suggested such a thing. George and Jon were whispering about where to buy the cases of wine. My mother was asleep, open-mouthed. Later, when she woke, I took her hand. "I had an interesting conversation with Ursula," I said. "I don't want to talk about it," she said.

We went on this way, avoiding. "We'll deal with it after the wedding," I reasoned, but called hospice anyway. At home I picked a dress, returned the rest. Jon and I settled on the cheapest catering we could find, an Indian restaurant that wound up giving us both indigestion.

My mother returned home days before the wedding, setting up once more in a rented bed in the sunroom. "Don't say *hospice,*" we told the nurses who came and went, bearing IV bags of comfort, patches of painkiller, dissolvable Dilaudid because she vomited anything she swallowed. "Don't tell her why you're here; she's still not ready." But I wanted her to be ready, and strong enough to know the truth: she was dying. I wanted her to be strong enough to answer the questions that stung from the sliding place inside me. But she lolled in silent space-time on her sweaty cot. She'd entered the hospital cancer-thin, all sinew and bone. But they pumped her full of saline, and now her body resembled an inflated plastic glove, translucent white and reaching.

The day before the wedding, friends arrived and camped out back, stinking of booze and bug spray and weed. My father carried boxes of wine and ferried people in from the airport. Jon's family arrived from California, grilled rehearsal dinner, sang karaoke, and showed up the next day wearing pressed linen. Through all this, my mother stayed shut in the sunroom like a secret, sleeping, resting up for the ceremony she was determined to attend. "Is it wrong that I just want this all to be over with?" I asked Jon one night, numb and exhausted. "Try to enjoy it," he said, looking hurt. "Let go, enjoy it," I repeated to myself each time I started to dread the wedding and the looming question of my mother's attendance. *Will she make it?* we all asked. Just walking to the bathroom had become a herculean feat. "Maybe we could FaceTime her in from the sunroom?" someone said. "Or film it and let her watch it later?"

Early morning on my wedding day. I woke with the sunrise to walk in the woods, looking for shafts of light. Inside, my mother had risen, too. Judy and her other close friend of forty years, Penelope, corralled her into the downstairs bathroom to wash her hair and dress her in the only outfit that would fit her suddenly corpulent body — a pair of silk PJ pants I'd given her the Christmas before, and a long beaded jacket. In the hours before the ceremony they dressed her, let her rest, held the pink tub for her while she vomited, little tears gathering in the corners of her eyes.

■ ■ ■ ■

A stylist arrived to do my hair; my girl-friends gathered in my mother's empty bedroom, which had become for that night the room I would share with Jon. We popped champagne, took pictures. Rain arrived to flood the garden, and we watched from the upstairs window as guests retreated to the dinner tent, with the overwhelming smell of curry wafting over from the Indian buffet, the awkwardly assembled sound system, the laser light show that zigzagged across the canvas ceiling in fluorescent purple and green.

In the mirror, I was not myself, primped and bridal, teetering on my too-high heels. I had wanted to look free and easy, not like the airbrushed brides on the covers of magazines, their princess dresses promising a perfection no life could match. But now I looked more like them than myself, masked in makeup and an intricate updo. There was nothing I could do about it. I grabbed my bouquet and descended the stairs.

"If you want to see your mother, now is the time," Judy said, and I followed her into the sunroom, unsure of what I'd find. Maybe Mary had magically transformed, as she had so many times before, to the mother of my childhood, protective and strong. But I found her unfamiliar, rouged like a corpse, her tumid ankles peeking out, inflated and purple. "My little girl," she said, suddenly lucid, suddenly herself, as I leaned over her bed, saying, "Mommy," repeating the word to calm the blood pounding in my torso, my head. I was exhausted. I wanted only to curl in bed beside her, melt into her body as I did in my childhood. But I withdrew, afraid of ruining my makeup. Then she was gone, swept away by a bevy of friends and nurses, who carried her distended form to her seat in the tent.

I looked at her there, during the ceremony, and wondered if she was looking back at me or if she was simply gazing through me, toward the shadowy distance ahead of her. I looked back at Jon, swearing to be my heart's companion, its protector, its equal in all things, and thought him beautiful, made more so by the yellow light of the tent, the storm beating at its outer walls.

In the weeks that followed, my first weeks of marriage, after friends and family left, after my mother returned to the hospital, Judy and I returned to caretaking. Jon waited patiently outside my mother's room while we leaned over her, fiddling with the malfunctioning G-tube. Some days during a lull in the vomiting or the tube leakage, I put my ear to the door of her room. Was she sleeping? Staring into space? She rarely spoke, afraid she'd vomit if she did.

"Did she say anything?" I'd ask anyone who went in her room without me. Usually it was Jon, who sat with her each day, reading to her or sometimes just holding her hand. "Not really," he'd say, and I'd stomp off, frustrated with her for not addressing the obvious. Death was unutterable to her even as it approached. But I wanted to hear her say it. "I don't want to talk about it," she'd murmur when Judy or I tried to broach the subject.

Sometimes, though, when a group was gathered, she'd hold court, Mother Mary speaking painkiller gibberish while I made notes in my phone, scrolling through them later, trying to decipher a hidden code. She talked about Edith's mansion — *Every Sunday flowers arrive, each one a different message* — and her childhood bedroom — *A crack in the ceiling where the fairy was trapped.* She talked about my father — *Here's the shadow of a man. Who is it? George?* — and she talked, I think, about me — *Chicky gets off the plane and goes straight to the hospital.*

But the closest she ever got to talking about death was with Jon. "At least she'll have some freedom," she said out of nowhere, holding his hand. He nodded along, not knowing what she meant. But I did.

Time slowed down. Nurses came and went. She slept on the patio, sun on her face.

33

My mother's last meal was the Jell-O we served her on her birthday in March. Her last words to me were "I love you, go go." She died on a Tuesday, the first day of September, alone in her bed in the sun-room. Judy was already up, in the garden. Jon, Richard, and I were still sleeping. For days we'd waited, sitting with her voiceless body, from which her spirit waned in stages, her breath like breaking waves, the ocean echoing through the curl of a conch shell.

We'd spoken to her, held her hand, told her we were there, to rest, to let go. The nurses had lifted the sheets to show me her body, mottling in shades of yellow, turning cold with the weather, the shortening summer days. Even so, I hadn't believed it, not until I felt her lifeless body, finally free of itself. Not until I kissed her cheek, touched her unresponsive hand, then signed the paperwork to permit the man in the black

SUV to wheel her away. And even then.

Even *now* I expect to hear her voice, receive her call. I look for her words everywhere. In her memoirs, the binders of her writing I read obsessively, and in the old journals I scour, or our old emails about nothing at all. I send text messages to her number, still saved to the Favorites section of my phone, knowing she won't respond. And still I crave her voice, her protection. I crave her assurance that somehow, through writing her story, Midge's story, my story, I can save myself from the curse. Our words will free us, my mother believed. Through them we can assume the magic that must be our mantle, in a world determined upon our silence.

Six months after her death I consult a medium who sees a garden and asks about my mother's book. "Your mother will visit you in dreams," she says. "She already does," I tell her, not mentioning how dark they are, how tinted with madness, these visitations I both look forward to and fear.

In them I meet my mother, broken and confused, not living but not yet dead. One night I find her corpse, forgotten in a bedroom, then realize she is still alive. She rises, vampiric, from her bed, holding her arms out to me, asking for embrace, and I am elated, repulsed, and finally unable to tell her she's not alive. The next night she is beautiful. The next night she is lost. The next night I watch her walk confidently out onto a bridge that will not hold, then fall into a ravine. When I peer over the cliff's edge I see her body, small and contorted on the snowy ground. I run to save her, to protect her, to lift the whole of her, broken and unconscious, in the cradle of my arms. I walk back up the cliffside.

Always in these dreams is the shadow of the conversation we never had. "Can we talk about what is going to happen to you?" I ask her one night. We are at a restaurant, eating Jell-O in our nightgowns. She looks down. She might cry. *Yes,* she says, *of course.* I am aware, in the moment, that I already know what her death will look like. The dream ends there. We never have the conversation.

Sometimes I can almost hear her in my head. The medium said this *was* her, but I'm skeptical. I think it may be me instead. Or perhaps it is both of us, perhaps when I thought she'd lost her voice, I was wrong.

Perhaps her silence was a gift — her voice, to me.

This is, I realize, the best I can hope for, this inner mother voice. This is the voice I must channel for the rest of my life, as my mother did before me, imagining Midge every birthday and Christmas, every time she felt lost.

At night, afraid of dreams, I lie awake and consider motherhood, the daughter I could have. The prospect of parenthood seems impossible without Mary. But I have always pictured myself the mother of a daughter, perhaps because the relationship with my mother was the most important of my life. I was so intrinsically her child, her girl. I was bound to her. For everything I can't remember, for everything I've lost, I feel that sense of oneness like a phantom limb. It is almost unbelievable that a woman so marked by her own mother's loss could bring herself so fully to her child's life. And yet it happens all the time, doesn't it?

"I have never been so grounded," Mary told me once when I asked her how it felt to be pregnant. She sounded self-possessed and sure, her voice colored by the confidence she reserved almost exclusively for when she spoke about me and how happy I would be, how safe in my marriage and my life. It was the same sureness she brought to our conversations about the LeRoy girls. "I know," she said, "I know I know I know." Looking back, I'm glad I let her stay so sure. Because I need to remember her this way, this strong. I need to believe she was unafraid to leave me and that I will make it without her, that my love will make it, that my writing will make it; that I will be half the mother she was, that if my daughter disappears beneath the weight of womanhood, if she loses her voice to tics or tragedy, I will have the power to call her back again.

SOURCES

Abbott, Megan E. *The Fever: A Novel.* New York: Back Bay Books/Little, Brown and Company, 2015.

Belluscio, Lynne J. *LeRoy.* Charleston, SC: Arcadia Publishing, 2010.

Belson, Ken. "Upstate, Where It Was First Made, Unwavering Devotion to Jell-O." *New York Times,* May 4, 2008. nytimes.com/2008/05/04/nyregion/04jello.html.

Bonenti, Charles. "A Portrait of Norman Rockwell." *Berkshire Eagle,* May 21, 2014. berkshireeagle.com/stories/a-portrait-of-norman-rockwell,373086.

Celebrating 100 Years of Jell-O. Lincolnwood, IL: Publications International, 1997.

Cixous, Hélène, and Catherine Clément. *The Newly Born Woman.* Minneapolis: University of Minnesota Press, 1986.

Denny, Dianna. "Classic Ads: Norman Rockwell, Ad Man." *Saturday Evening*

Post, May 11, 2012. saturdayeveningpost
.com/2012/05/11/art-entertainment/nor
man-rockwell-art-entertainment/norman-
rockwell-ad-man.html.

Dominus, Susan. "What Happened to the Girls in LeRoy." *New York Times Magazine,* March 7, 2012. nytimes.com/2012/03/11/magazine/teenage-girls-twitching-leroy.html.

Estrin, Robin. "Neighbors Raise a Stink About Jell-O Factory." *Los Angeles Times,* February 29, 1996. articles.latimes.com/1996-02-29/business/fi-41535_1_plant-tour.

Freud, Sigmund, and Josef Breuer. *Studies in Hysteria.* Nicola Luckhurst (translator). London: Penguin, 2004.

Friedan, Betty. *The Feminine Mystique.* New York: W. W. Norton, 1963.

Gilman, Sander L., Helen King, Roy Porter, G. S. Rousseau, and Elaine Showalter. *Hysteria Beyond Freud.* Berkeley: University of California Press, 1993.

Grey, Sarah. "A Social History of Jell-O Salad: The Rise and Fall of an American Icon." *Serious Eats,* August 2015. serious eats.com/2015/08/history-of-jell-o-salad.html.

Hari, Vani Deva. "This Childhood Favorite Has a Warning Label in Europe — Why

Not Here?" *Food Babe,* October 11, 2016. foodbabe.com/2014/05/21/this-childhood-favorite-has-a-warning-label-in-europe-why-not-here/.

"The History of Jell-O." jellogallery.org/history.html.

Howe, Katherine. *Conversion.* London: Rock the Boat, 2015.

"Jell-O Company." nyhistoric.com/2014/01/jell-o-company/.

Joys of Jell-O Gelatin Dessert. White Plains, NY: General Foods, 1963.

Kim, Kyle, Christina Littlefield, and Mark Olsen. "Bill Cosby: A 50-Year Chronicle of Accusations and Accomplishments." *Los Angeles Times,* April 26, 2016. latimes.com/entertainment/la-et-bill-cosby-timeline-htmlstory.html.

Lawson, Carol. "Anorexia — It's Not a New Disease." *New York Times,* December 8, 1985. nytimes.com/1985/12/08/style/anorexia-it-s-not-a-new-disease.html.

Malone, Noreen, and Amanda Demme. " 'I'm No Longer Afraid': 35 Women Tell Their Stories About Being Assaulted by Bill Cosby, and the Culture That Wouldn't Listen." *The Cut, New York,* July 26, 2015. thecut.com/2015/07/bill-cosbys-accusers-speak-out.html.

Miller, Arthur. *The Crucible: A Play in Four*

Acts. New York: Viking, 1953.

The New Joys of Jell-O: Recipe Book. White Plains, NY: General Foods, 1975.

Rich, Adrienne. *Of Woman Born: Motherhood as Experience and Institution.* New York: W. W. Norton, 1976.

Rodale, Maria. "Food as Medicine: How One Hospital Is Using Organic Produce to Help Heal Patients." *Huffington Post,* September 30, 2014. huffingtonpost.com/maria-rodale/food-as-medicine-how-one-_b_5637961.html.

"School Baffled by 12 Girls' Mystery Symptoms." *The Today Show,* NBC. January 18, 2012.

Schultz, E. J. "Kraft Launches Comeback Plan for Jell-O." *Advertising Age,* August 12, 2013. adage.com/article/news/ kraft-launches-campaign-revive-jell-o/243616/.

Shapiro, Laura. *Perfection Salad.* New York: Random House, 2001.

Stradley, Linda. "History of Gelatin, Gelatine, and Jell-O." *What's Cooking America,* February 9, 2017. whatscookingamerica.net/History/Jell-0-history.htm.

"Teens Suffer from Mystery Illness." *Dr. Drew on Call,* HLN. December 3, 2012.

The Town That Caught Tourette's. The Learning Channel. May 10, 2013.

Usdin, Steven T. "The Rosenberg Archive:

A Historical Timeline." *The Cold War International History Project.* The Woodrow Wilson International Center for Scholars, July 7, 2009. wilsoncenter.org/publication/ the-rosenberg-archive-historical-timeline.

Watters, Ethan. "The Americanization of Mental Illness." *New York Times Magazine,* January 8, 2010. nytimes.com/2010/01/10/ magazine/ 10psyche-t.html.

Wyman, Carolyn. *Jell-O: A Biography.* San Diego: Harcourt, 2001.

ACKNOWLEDGMENTS

Carolyn Wyman, in her brilliant history of Jell-O, *Jell-O: A Biography,* provided me with much of the history of America's most famous dessert found in these pages. I am greatly indebted to her, and to Laura Shapiro, whose *Perfection Salad* educated me extensively about the origins and rationale behind the domestic-science movement. Ditto Susan Dominus, whose 2012 *New York Times Magazine* essay "What Happened to the Girls in LeRoy" was not only the single most thorough and insightful piece of reportage about the girls, but it was also the first article sent to me by my mother as she prodded me to start this book. Thank you to these three brilliant writers, and to all the other sources I drew from as I worked on *Jell-O Girls.*

Thank you to my teachers: Mat Johnson, who urged me to write this book and gave me the deadlines I needed to do so; Pete

Turchi, who read and commented and made himself endlessly available to my anxious questions; Nick Flynn, who inspired my early writing and my first years in the program at the University of Houston, to which I am also greatly indebted. Thank you to *Inprint* for their generous financial support as I wrote, and *Tin House* for offering me the scholarship that helped me finish.

Thank you to Maggie Nelson, whose mentorship and correspondence over my MFA and PhD years have given me confidence and clarity. Thank you to Janet Sarbanes for always giving close reads, invaluable advice, and the very warmest encouragement to keep going. Thanks also to the MFA program at the California Institute of the Arts, and my teachers there, Maggie and Janet, Mady Schutzman, and Jon Wagner. I have never been so happy and inspired and alive in language as I was during my time at CalArts.

Thank you times a million to my brilliant lioness of an agent, Marya Spence, who understood this book and helped me to do the same. And to Carina Guiterman, editor extraordinaire, who urged me to name the curse, and to write ever closer to its undoing. Thank you to the whole team at Little, Brown for the joyous care you've given to me and to *Jell-O Girls* from the outset.

To Richard Mogavero — thank you for being my companion, and Mary's, in waiting rooms and kitchens, on wooded dog walks and errand runs. Thank you for endless cups of tea, endless dinners, movies, music — thank you, most of all, for being my Unkie.

Thank you to Ariella Rojhani, Penelope Bodry Sanders and Mack Goode, Jane Hesford, Marcia Gamble, Ray Walker, Ashley Wurzbacher, Emily Kiernan, Liz Hall, Amanda Montei, Sarah McClung, Cecile Just, Nicholas Katzban, Marco DiDomenico, "Team Jo Ann Beard," all my other angels, and all of Mary's angels — you know who you are.

To my father, George Rowbottom, who has come to the table with me on this book, line by line, bravely and with love, just as he came to my mother's front door after so many years, bravely, with love. Dad, your willingness to meet me here, in this new emotional space we've written, is one of the great gifts of my life.

To Judy Rasmuson: you have showed me what generosity means, you have showed me what sisterhood means, you have showed me what the future can look like, as we move forward into new memories together.

381

We were so lucky to have had Mary for so much of both our lives — we remain so lucky to have each other. I may never find the words to thank you for your presence in my life — but I'll keep trying.

And, last, to Jon, dearest beloved, heart, husband, friend. Thank you for all our dreams. For our great love. You have tended me like a plant. Without you I would be un-blossomed.

ABOUT THE AUTHOR

Allie Rowbottom received her BA from New York University, her MFA from the California Institute of the Arts, and her PhD in creative writing and literature from the University of Houston, where she was an Inprint Memorial Barthelme Fellow in nonfiction and was awarded the Marion Barthelme Prize in creative writing. Her work has received scholarships, essay prizes, and honorable mentions from *Tin House,* the Best American Essays series, the *Florida Review,* the *Bellingham Review,* the *Black Warrior Review,* the *Southampton Review,* and *Hunger Mountain.* She lives and writes in Los Angeles.

The employees of Thorndike Press hope you have enjoyed this Large Print book. All our Thorndike, Wheeler, and Kennebec Large Print titles are designed for easy reading, and all our books are made to last. Other Thorndike Press Large Print books are available at your library, through selected bookstores, or directly from us.

For information about titles, please call:
(800) 223-1244

or visit our website at:
gale.com/thorndike

To share your comments, please write:
Publisher
Thorndike Press
10 Water St., Suite 310
Waterville, ME 04901